Cover photo: archive
Home for the Relief of Suffering

Printed by:
Grafiche GRILLI srl – Foggia (Italy)
Via Manfredonia Km 2,200
Tel. 0039 0881 568040

To the Prayer groups
born from the heart of Padre Pio
may they treasure his memory and act in the
world as ferment of Christian life.

Fr. Marcellino IasenzaNiro

THE "PADRE"
SAINT PIO OF PIETRELCINA

His mission to save souls

TESTIMONIES

FIRST PART

EDIZIONI
PADRE PIO
DA PIETRELCINA

"Our Lady of Grace" Capuchin Friary
71013 San Giovanni Rotondo (FG) Italy 2006

Original title: "IL PADRE"
SAN PIO DA PIETRELCINA
La missione di salvare le anime
TESTIMONIANZE

Traslated into English by Patricia Anne MacKinlay

CONTENTS

INTRODUCTION

When Padre Pio was alive his spiritual children often talked about their experiences with him: "He said this to me, he behaved like this with me, he did this for me". Those who spoke did so spontaneously almost as a loving moral duty; those who listened were happy to hear what the others said.

The natural image of the Padre, not the one that came from writings which were often not accurate, spread in this way and was lodged in the heart, before the mind, and was treasured there as a true icon, inspired not by creative capabilities but from hearing that which came from the heart little as it may have seemed. Every saint is a "fact" given to the Church from Heaven and must be recognised and treasured.

The wish to know who Padre Pio was, or, better still, is, is to be found today stronger than ever amongst those who never had the chance to meet him: struck by this extraordinary figure of servant of God, they want to know from the witnesses who had the luck to live near to him or speak to him even just a few times, what he really did or said.

The request, for instance, from parish priests or directors of prayer groups, who often invite us to conferences or to visit their communities, to hear us talk about the Padre is always stimulated by this wish: "Tell us about the little things in his life", where "little" certainly does not mean banal or without meaning. People wish to be told about brief episodes, rich in details, which they can evaluate and comment on.

"The man of today", writes John Paul II in quoting from the *Evangelii Nuntiandi*, believes in witnesses more than teachers, in experience more than in doctrine, in life and facts more than in theories"[1].

Whoever talks to the spiritual children or admirers of our Saint realises that all the reflections about the figure of Padre Pio never catch the audience's attention as much as hearing testimonies, especially if they concern episodes of the speaker's life.

Being lucky enough to have known and lived with the Padre for a while; being one of the witnesses who testified during the beatification and canonization process, and who gave the Church, through their declarations, the documentation to raise Padre Pio to the altars, I have often been invited to talk about the Saint my confrère especially to prayer groups, but also to the faithful of parish churches and shrines during mission meetings or spiritual exercise courses. Here I found myself in front of the warmly felt request to give real firsthand knowledge and information.

Since I could not only speak of my memories, it was necessary to gather information for my speeches. Firstly I spoke to my confrères who lived with the Padre and to some spiritual children who live in San Giovanni Rotondo. Realising with wonder that our towns are still full of news about Padre Pio I took special care to note all that those who know the Padre or had been directly influenced in a spiritual way could tell me.

One of the witnesses I particularly counted on is Fr Pellegrino Funicelli, who lived with Padre Pio for fifteen years. From

---

[1]   *Redemptoris Missio*, n. 42.

the end of 1974 until October 1982 he collaborated monthly with the magazine *"Voce di Padre Pio"* writing articles gathered under the title "The teachings of Padre Pio" and "Padre Pio's guidance".

I have often drawn from these articles, mainly because they are documents that still have the scent of the atmosphere one could feel around Padre Pio when he was still among us and this greatly interested me. One day, not long before his death, which took place on 17 April 1988, I asked the dear brother why he hadn't written a book about Padre Pio; and he replied that he was going to sort out and gather together all that he had published in the magazine printed by the Friary of San Giovanni Rotondo. And he added: "There is all about Padre Pio as I saw him".

With regards to this book Fr. Pellegrino is useful through another source. He has left a good number of handwritten and typed files, loosely bound together, which he used to dictate reflections during the month of May 1976. The unpublished document will be quoted under the title *Marian Month*.

The material collected, first in San Giovanni Rotondo and later in many parts of Italy, from the voices of those who really "saw, listened to and touched him", have been useful to illustrate the figure of the Padre in carrying out his ministry of predication. The friends of our dear holy Confrère and the leaders and directors of the Padre Pio prayer groups prayed and begged me to make public and publish the notes I made for myself.

It was necessary to rewrite them, so that the work would have a united theme; and gradually as this took place I felt a need which pushed me onwards: a need to tell the story, that is to keep and conserve memories so that nothing of the admirable existence of Padre Pio would be lost. All dedicated to the Glory of God and to the good of the brothers.

Now the reader has the complete set of conferences and conversations at his disposition. What each one has in his hands certainly isn't the life of the holy Confrère in the true sense of the word – tracing the historic and spiritual adventure of a character, instead it records some important aspects of his personality.

I believe that more than the reflections, the testimonies will bring to the reader's mind the traces of an image both real and objective, showing signs which at a first glance could appear contradictory in a man of God. I refer to the strength and severity of the Saint demonstrated in his defence of the Christian values of the divine law and at the same time his ardent love for the people, twisted in body and spirit, who he met every day along his way and whom he aided.

His mission to save souls

One day during a Confession in which he was particularly provoked by Fr. Pellegrino about his many activities, Padre Pio declared: "My mission is that of saving souls. All the rest is of less importance. Therefore coming to confess to me you must neither distract yourself nor distract me from this intention"[2].

Padre Pio with this declaration gave me a trail to follow writing this book. As he carried out his mission mainly in the confessional, it is there that I looked as a reference point to present him as the minister of the Sacrament of Forgiveness.

The charismatic aspect of the Padre will stand out at the

---

[2]   *Marian Month*, day 14.

same time. Few of God's servants, in the Church's history have stirred up the same enthusiasm and interest that people reserved for Padre Pio. We must admit that the figure of this Saint became extraordinarily great in the minds of the people, because he, with the help of the Holy Spirit, could reveal the innermost secrets of the penitents, to whom he revealed faults they kept hidden, purposely or unknowingly – and work miracles that relieved those in suffering or troubled.

The charisms of the Holy Spirit exerted by Padre Pio have been carefully taken into consideration, not only to underline the fact that these gifts are a part of the set of means which the Lord gives to his servants to carry their missions, but also to show all the Saint of Pietrelcina's humanity. He was always involved with the pain and suffering of his brothers and sisters, for whom he became the Good Samaritan. This happened not only in the confessional but also when he moved within the church and Friary while the people crowded around at his passing.

The reader will become aware that the areas, in which the Saint worked, are not only those of the Capuchin Friary, a solitary place on the Gargano, where Jesus had fixed him to a cross: the Holy Spirit enabled him to become like a shadow for those who had returned in the Grace of God, to accompany them, follow them and help them even from a distance.

Padre Pio would be the Good Shepherd who went looking for the lost sheep, unknown to him because he had never met it, to take it back safely to the pen.

All this took place through the Holy Spirit, but the Saint conformed with his actions, giving himself totally. Often many people when referring to the venerable Padre, intent on bringing people into God's Grace, have in mind a minister of God who incarnates the role of a hard to please strict judge. This only matches one side of the truth. To Fr. Pellegrino, who in a certain sense reproved his severity and strictness he answered: "It's true I make my penitents sweat blood. But I also add my own blood"[3].

To help Padre Pio carry out his great mission, Our Lady of Grace was there, who accompanied him not only in the confessional but also on the altar where he sacrificed himself with Jesus, a victim of atonement.

Suffering in agony day after day for the well-being of many souls, Padre Pio became the father of many spiritual children, who felt him as such, who when they spoke about him called him: the "Padre"(Father).

For us brothers in the Friary he was our "spiritual father" and we didn't know how else to call him, after knowing his love, which even our parents were not able to give us because they were bound by human limits. He, no, he never disappointed our expectations, when we trusted him with our physical and spiritual health, our studies and our vocations, because in his breast Christ's heart was beating.

With these pages I wish to express my thanks to Padre Pio to whom I entrusted my priesthood, before the Lord made me gift of so many blessings.

San Giovanni Rotondo, 21 February 2004.

---

[3]   *Marian Month*, day 9.

HIS MISSION TO SAVE SOULS

I. A SINGULAR CONFESSOR

Pope John Paul II, in the homily of the Mass which celebrated Padre Pio's canonization said about him: "He was a generous dispenser of divine mercy, making it available to all through his welcome, spiritual guidance and especially by his administration of the Sacrament of Penance". He then indicated the new Saint as a model for priests to imitate: "May his example encourage priest to carry out their ministry which is so important, with joy and diligence"[4].

Yes, Padre Pio must be looked to by the priests as an example to refer to. And not only as a minister of the Sacrament of Reconciliation. Fr. Pellegrino Funicelli in a conference held at San Giovanni Rotondo, after the Padre's death said: "One day during a break, in the garden, people were talking of the mission of the saints God sent to earth, saying: "this one came for this reason, that one for this other". The Padre listened and took part, then as the discussion drifted away from the theme, the Saint appeared to be distant and locked in his thoughts.

At a certain moment Mario Sanvico said: "Well Padre, every man, not only the saints, comes to earth to carry out a mission. What mission have you come for?"

Padre Pio replied: "I have come for the priests".

---

[4]   The Osservatore Romano, 17-18th June 2002.

Our holy confrère, brought to the attention of all, placing them on high, the Eucharist, Confession and obedience to the Church. We must be blind if we can't see this. By his example Padre Pio invited every priest to put this reality on the altar of their heart and brain[5].

1. The Confession crisis

We believe that the invitation to the priests by the Pope, to imitate Padre Pio during the Sacrament of Penance, sprang from the observation that a growing number of the faithful no longer confess or do so rarely. This is a reality that can be seen by all.

What are the causes? Among the many the secularization and de-consecration of the world; that is, man, during his life, no longer refers to God and to the unchangeable laws given by the Creator to his creatures, so that they may control their actions following the Lord's guide to carry out their idea and plans.

St. Thomas Aquinas teaches us to see in the divine precepts "a dimension that structures the human being in itself and steers and stimulates his development"[6].

Unfortunately, in the laws given by the Creator, man sees only something that halts and limits his liberty. Therefore he does not accept them. And from this refusal to be guided by God, comes the sin which St. Augustine defines as "an expression or fact or any desire which clashes with the eternal law"[7].

---

[5]   The title of the conference was "The priesthood of Padre Pio" and it was held by the Capuchin Friars on 18th April 1985. Fr. Pellegrino states that the lawyer Santoro of Rome gave him this testimony.

[6]   THOMAS AQUINAS, *Summa Teologica*, I-II, q. 106, a. l.

[7]   *Nuovo dizionario di spiritualità*, edited by Stefano De Flores and Tullio Goffi, Ed. Paoline 1979, 1193.

Speaking of sin, even with regards to priests we can see the aspect of offending the Creator is often underlined. Without doubt an offence takes place, its malice is in the ingratitude of man towards God who has filled him with gifts and enriched his very being with his will, his intellect and his ability to love in the lack of confidence and doubt that He is really in the right in what He does and says: in disobedience and rebellion, that is a deliberate act of challenge: and finally in his refusal to be involved in a project of love and salvation. In truth God invites man to a royal banquet, the Word states: *"Blessed are those who are invited to the marriage supper of the Lamb"* (Ap 19,9).

But looking at man's refusal of God, he does not consider enough the loss and harm this causes the sinner.

If we examine the etymon of *peccatum*, we can see that this word, as well as fault and offence also means error and "mistake with more or less heavy consequences, the effect of which falls upon those who made it".

In the Old Testament, amongst the main expressions used to indicate sin, we find '*Hatta'*, which means "to miss the aim, not to find what one is looking for, to make a false move".

Man who sins, therefore, is like an arrow that misses the mark; so whilst he wishes to create autonomous alternatives of salvation and happiness, too often he finds himself in misfortune, because he lives in a state of alienation for himself; in fact he was created by God and for God, sin, which breaks his relationship with his Creator tends to disintegrate his own human personality.

What happens next is easily verifiable: in him we can find conditions of stress and disappointment, a violent craving an insatiable desire for other goods that should fill an emptiness that instead remains impossible to fill. Necessarily also the so-

cial effects involved: the relationship with his fellowmen of
who lives in this state cannot be constructive. Conditioned by
a state of mind that is certainly not that of a free man, he will
lean towards satisfying his own egoism rather than take note
of the rights of others.

Therefore the worst evil for man is sin!

Nowadays however *evil* is not seen in sin, but it is indicated
in other elements, which are always negative such as illness,
war, hunger, pollution and social injustice. No matter how
much man busies himself to try and resolve these grave problems, if in the plans to eliminate the causes, naturally those
within human capabilities, there is no place for God, not only
is there no remedy, but the problems worsen.

John Paul II returning from Canada where he had enjoyed
the opportunity to be once more among his young people in
the World Youth Day, during the Sunday *Angelus*, said to the
crowds who greeted him in St. Peter's Square: "A world that
does hold Christ as a reference, is a world that sooner or later,
ends against man. The history of a past, also recent, shows this.
One cannot reject God without then having to reject man"[8].

Padre Pio at the possibility of yielding to an evil instinct
which is in every man and break the divine law by sinning,
trembled all over his body. He wrote to his spiritual directors:
"I should prefer death a thousand times rather than to deliberately offend such a good God"[9]. And again: "I were to offend
God even in a single instance, I would prefer to suffer an infi-

---

[8]   The Osservatore Romano. 5-6th August 2002.

[9]   Padre Pio Da Pietrelcina, *Letters I, Correspondence with his spiritual
directors*, edited by Melchiorre da Pobladura and Alessandro da Ripabottoni, Edizioni "Padre Pio da Pietrelcina", Our Lady of Grace Friary, San
Giovanni Rotondo (FG), 1971, 213. 223. 909.

nite number of times the most agonizing martyrdom"[10].

At the sight of the sin that he saw in the world the Saint was dismayed and expressed to Fr. Agostino from San Marco in Lamis great apprehension, regret and sorrow:

"I won't stop weeping during all the hours I still have to live, for you know how it rends my heart to see so many poor blind souls who flee more quickly than they would from fire when they hear the divine Masters' more tender invitation: *If anyone thirsts, let him come to me and drink* (Jn 7, 37). I am very distressed when I consider these really blind people who have no pity for themselves because their passions have blunted their judgement to such an extent that they do not even dream of coming to drink this true water of paradise.

Observe how the enemies of the cross are emerging more and more triumphant every day…, they burn continually with living fire amid a thousand desires for earthly pleasures…

Divine compassion does not touch them; they are not attracted by benefits; they are not checked by punishments; when treated gently are insolent; in face of severity they are furious ; when things go well with them they become puffed up; in adversity they despair"[11].

To the same father he wrote:

"…You understand what a cruel torment my soul endures at the sight of the enormous offences committed by the sons of men in these most sad times"[12].

Man having lost the sense of sin, it is natural that the Sacra-

---

[10] *Ibid.*, 1053: 26th September 1917.

[11] *Ibid.*, 744-745; 10th October 1915.

[12] *Ibid.*, 754: 17th October 1915.

ment of Reconciliation, Confession, would suffer a crisis. Often the faithful, unless they have done something particularly grave, ask: "What must I confess?" Some, even after years away from the Sacrament of Penance, when asked what the things are which are troubling their conscience, answered: "I have done nothing wrong".

We are in a total loss of morals.

Pio XII had warned: "Perhaps the greatest sin nowadays is that men have started to lose the sense of sin"[13]. And Paul VI, twenty years later agreed with what his predecessor predicted: "You will no longer find in today's language, in books, in things that talk about men, the tremendous word sin. It never comes up. And it will not return because once human mind has separated from the divine wisdom the concept of sin has been lost"[14].

One could feel lost and lose hope, but the Lord does not abandon His people and His aid comes as only He knows.

St. Teresa Benedicta of the Cross, Edith Stein, wrote in the Christmas of 1940: "The deeper an age is plunged in sin, and distant from God, the greater is the need for souls who are united to him. Even in these circumstances he makes sure these souls are present: during the darkest nights the greatest saints and prophets are born"[15].

Padre Pio is one of these great souls sent by God to bring light to humanity. Here is the news of the first meeting of this Saint with God's people.

"Crowds of people thirsting for Jesus are pressing upon me,

---

[13]   Radio message VIII Catechistic Congress, USA 1946.

[14]   Homily XVIII Whitsunday 1964.

[15]   E. GARCIA ROJO, *Edith Stein, Patrona d'Europa*, in *Rivista di vita spirituale*, March-April 2002, 185.

so I am at my wit's end", he wrote from Foggia on 23 August 1916 to Fr. Agostino of San Marco in Lamis, his confessor, apologising for not having sent him any news, and added: "Please don't blame me…I am not left a free moment"[16].

It is to be noted that the Padre had only been in the town of Foggia for a few months, he arrived on 17 February to spiritually aid the noblewoman Raffaelina Cerase, who was gravely ill and who flew to Heaven on 25 March of the same year. He was not yet Padre Pio with the stigmata: an oil lamp placed on a candelabrum, on a mountain to make light and call the people.

What happened later at San Giovanni Rotondo is written in the few lines by the Padre in a letter to his other spiritual father, Fr. Benedetto Nardella of san Marco in Lamis, who complained he had been neglected by the young priest, who was "reluctant to keep up relation" by letter which the director considered "necessary": "It is now one o'clock in the morning as I pen these few lines. I have been working for nineteen hours without a break"[17].

We are in 1919.

With reference to this year, a note in the Chronicle of the Friary of San Giovanni Rotondo confirmed what the Padre wrote to his provincial father, Fr. Benedetto;

"It was a striking scene to see the square of the Friary, and the area nearby packed with people who were waiting to enter the church, also crowded; and from every direction came cars, carriages, carts, gigs and sledges.

The wait could go on for days, as it is not difficult to imagine.

---

16 Letters I, 896.
17 Ibid., 1291: 16.11.1919.

Padre Pio confessed tirelessly from morning to evening. Sometimes he remained in the confessional for eighteen hours without a break. The carabinieri (police) had to be called to give a hand in regulating the entrance into the church and to discipline the flow of people to the Padre's confessional.

Something similar happened in the sacristy, where Padre Pio confessed the men, before going into the church.

People came not only from Italy; but, not in crowds of course, also from other Countries"[18].

However it was in his role as a confessor that the Padre during his lifetime was always brought into discussion by those who were unable to carefully observe his scrupulous minister in the Sacrament of Reconciliation.

Mgr. Edward Nowak, secretary of the Congregation for the Causes of Saints, in some of the personal memories he gave to the *Osservatore Romano*, a month after the canonization of Padre Pio of Pietrelcina, noted that one of the reasons why the process did not proceed "at full speed towards the winning post of the beatification" was that the Inquiry was not "without difficulties" such as "that so called grumpy character" of the Capuchin which sometimes caused him to raise his voice in the confessional with some penitent, in front of other faithful waiting to confess[19].

2. Padre Pio controversial confessor

All those who lived or came to San Giovanni Rotondo, nat-

---

[18]   Chronicle of the Friary of San Giovanni Rotondo, manuscript, p. 25.
[19]   The *Osservatore Romano*, issue of 15-16th July 2002, 6.

urally we are speaking of those in good faith and not who were biased, soon realised that Padre Pio was someone out of the ordinary with regards to virtue and therefore leaning towards sainthood.

Despite this impression, many were unable to associate that positive image, both immediate and instantaneous, seen in an even brighter way if they had seen him pray and most of all celebrate Mass, with the terrible abusive speech he had when faced with sin sitting in the confessional.

They remained rather bewildered, as if the Saint, who had to resemble Jesus in his way of acting, had to imitate the Master only in gentleness and not in those strong reproves, even violent, that we find He made in the Gospels. Or as if the abusive speech against rich egoists, hypocrites or false just men, which burst out from Christ's heart was not an expression of love towards those who were in the wrong and who He wished to make in any way come to their senses.

For this reason those who shared Padre Pio's daily life, seeing the uneasiness shown by the penitents turned away from the confessional in a strong brusque way, were driven to discuss this with him. The subject of the method used by the Padre in the Confession could become a talking point even in the little break that he shared with his Brothers and friends. One evening the discussion was about St. Leopoldo Mandic, a Capuchin friar who passed all day confessing in the church of the Capuchins in Padua. Angelo Battisti, the administrator of the Home for the Relief of Suffering asked:

"Father, Fr. Leopoldo said that during his life he had refused to give absolution only twice and that he had regretted it".

And Padre Pio remained silent for a few moments then said: "When I refuse to give absolution I do not regret it as if one comes to me for Confession with firm belief, the non-absolution will teach him to be more careful in the future, if instead he comes to Confession without firm belief, the non-absolution does him good, because it brings him back to the reality of his situation and saves him from making a sacrilegious Confession"[20].

Padre Pio's heart divided between God and his brothers

With regards to his way of behaviour, which was not always accepted, already as a young priest Padre Pio had to give some explanations to his spiritual father Fr. Benedetto Nardella, who in a letter of 16 November 1921, clearly referring to the energy with which the Saint administered the Sacrament of Penance, says he was always waiting to receive "before long the news of complete victory" on *Lady gentleness*[21].

Padre Pio in his reply puts some preliminary remarks, which are the key to understand not only his way of acting but to enter into his soul. "I am devoured by the love of God and the love of my neighbour…" as if to make him could he understand that during confession these two loves tyrannized him to such a point to make him sometimes appear agitated, in wanting to defend now one now the other; then he explaines:

"Please believe me, father, when I tell you that my occasional outbursts are caused precisely by this harsh prison, even if you like to call it a happy one.

How is it possible to see God saddened by evil and not be

[20]   *Chronicle…*, p. 478: 17.12.1957.
[21]   Cf. *Letters* I, 1390: 16.11.1921.

saddened likewise? To see God on the point of letting fly his thunderbolts? To parry them there is no other remedy than to raise one hand to restrain his arm and with the other hand beckon urgently to one of the brother's for a twofold reason: that they may cast evil aside and move away at once from where they stand, since the Judge's hand is about to come down on them".

He however reassures his spiritual father that the Spirit was not even lightly touched by indignation and anger, two sentiments that the Apostle Paul did not justify in any Christian (cf. Ef 4,31).

"Please believe me, though, when I tell you that at such moments I am by no means shaken or changed in the depths of my soul. I feel nothing except the desire to have and to want what God wants. In him I always feel at rest, at least internally, while I am sometimes rather uncomfortable externally".

He ends his letter, showing his spiritual father those bonds that unite to those that he met on his way as good Samaritan:
"For my brothers? Alas! How often, not to say always, I have to say to God the Judge, with Moses: *either forgive them or else blot me out of the book of life.*

What a nasty thing it is to live by the heart! It means living at every moment a death that never kills, or experience a living death and a dying life.

Alas! Who will set me free from this consuming fire?[22].

---

[22] Cf. *Letters I*, 1393: 20.11.1921.

Like Jesus

Fr. Carmelo Durante too, Superior of the Friary of San Giovanni Rotondo in the fifties, gives us important details about
the subject.

One day, with great tact, talking to him like a son he asked
Padre Pio the reason for his apparent harshness, which he dis-
played in Confession. God's good servant after reaffirming
that his behaviour was only motivated by the charity which
bond him to his brothers enticed by sin, replied that his model
whom he referred to was the Divine Master: "I act in such a
way, because my heart of father wants to recall souls to penance! It can't bear that they remain in sin! I do with the sinners
what Jesus did with the Scribes and Pharisees.

They need to be called to conversion, to penance! And when
the good manners are no use, you need to be strict to wake
them up from the lethargy of sin and vice"[23].

In another circumstance he said to him: *"Listen, I treat people how they deserve before God"*[24].

Fr. Carmelo did not doubt in the least the Padre's correct-
ness, but just to be certain and to find answers for the others, he
once again approached the subject of the refusal of absolution,
speaking of it to the Saint who said: "Ok, let's talk about this
thorny and painful subject: the most painful for someone who
has faith.

Listen, my son, I use this system with certain souls – the
recidivist- to shake them, because especially for some kind of
sins it is easy to go from Confession to the sin and from the sin

---

[23] FR. CARMELO DURANTE, *Testimonianze*, I, 147 (typescript). Provincial
Archive of the Capuchins, Foggia.

[24] FR. CARMELO DURANTE, *Padre Pio, uomo santo di Dio*, edited by Fr.
Domenico Serini, Ed. Pugliesi, Martina Franca (TA) 2002, 78.

back to the Confession: one sins, confesses and is absolved, then one sins again, confesses and is absolved...; it becomes a routine, a custom...

Now, instead, the soul that is not absolved undergoes a spiritual trauma: this is one of the reasons. Here is the second: in this way the soul is really driven to follow the straight and narrow path and to start using all the means available to obtain redemption.

One could object that sometimes the penitent may fail to return. And also in this case I ask myself if it is better to make the penitents used to sin and to a Confession that would actually be sacrilegious, either for lack of purpose or repentance, or to make them aware they are in God's disgrace. I prefer the latter"[25].

Fr. Carmelo himself calls our attention to some events which had rather shocked him.

One day, late in the morning, he went out of his room to say hello to the Saint who was going to go back to the Friary, after confessing some women in the little church. Soon after, he saw him enter the centre corridor of the Friary in between two men. However one of them stopped whilst the other stayed by the Saint's side, humbly speaking to him.

When the Padre reached the threshold of cell n.1, the person he was speaking to fell to his knees and became more insistent about what he was explaining or pleading for. Suddenly Padre Pio started to shout: "When you don't wish to stop offending God, what do you come here for? Go away! Go away!".

So the poor man, who was still on his knees, humiliated and distressed after this harsh reproach, raising his voice up said:

---

[25] *Ibid.*, 111.

"But father, I didn't do anything, I'm innocent: the one who made the mistake is him, the one there in the background. It has nothing to do with me and yet you are shouting at me".

But the Padre, not at all pacified by this just comment continued in a loud voice saying "I know, I know that the sinner is the one over there in the background. That is why I am shouting, so that he can hear me" and with a threatening look at the friend who had prudently kept his distance, distinctly said "with the tone of voice of a prophet from the Old Testament": "You are an unrepentant sinner. Poor you! But beware of God's justice".

Soon afterwards he gently blessed the man who was still at his feet trembling and crying, then he went into his room, followed by the Father Guardian Fr. Carmelo, who was quite disconcerted and thoughtful.

As soon as they were alone, Padre Pio realising how upset he was said: "My son, to rouse certain souls you need cannonballs. Treating them with gentleness is a waste of time. They need to feel God's anger when the strength of his mercy is not enough. To tell the truth, writes Fr. Carmelo, there was nothing to object to in this pastoral comment, but those who that day as in many others, only thought about how Padre Pio's behaviour appeared to be, were tempted to think badly of his evangelical charity"[26].

Our confrère tells of another episode in which he was present which allows us to look deeper into Padre Pio's soul.

He had heard the Saint give another scolding in a loud voice, near cell n. 5. The Padre was reprimanding someone who had gone close to him, for his bad behaviour. Soon after this harsh

---

[26] Fr. Carmelo Durante, *Testimonianze…*, I, 156.

lecture, he turned calm and smiling towards Fr. Carmelo as if nothing had happened. The Superior rather amazed said: But father, how is it possible! A moment ago it seemed like the end of the world and now it's all changed. How can you explain it?".

The Padre with gentleness and humility, almost afraid that he had shocked his Father Guardian said: "My son, I was upset only at the surface, at skin level but inside, in my heart, I am always very calm and very serene, because here, he continued whilst touching his chest, is God". And touching his chest again with the fingertips of his right hand he kept on repeating as in a refrain: "God is in here, God is in here"[27].

Once he had carried out his duties with the spiritual charity needed, either in the confessional or where the Holy Spirit wanted him to work, the Saint returned back in his normal state of quiet and meditation.

The exterior display of agitation he showed in his moments of reprehension, never ever touched his heart.

So as we have seen, in correcting he could refer to Jesus, the perfect example he always desired to imitate.

Worries and opinions of the spiritual children

Padre Pio's spiritual daughters were also afraid that perhaps he was too strict. "One day, recounted one of these, who with others were around Padre Pio, we said to him: "Father, you shouldn't treat people badly otherwise they won't come anymore". He replied: "I act as they do at harvest time: they beat the sheaves to separate the wheat from the straw. Then they

---

[27] *Ibid.*, 154-155.

winnow the wheat to eliminate the straw and leave the wheat behind"[28].

The Saint, comparing himself to the farm worker who winnows the wheat, couldn't have given a better example to make us understand how much thought and care he used during the Sacrament of Penance. Jesus Himself was introduced by John the Baptist as He who had the fan in his hands to gather the wheat into his granary and leave the chaff to its destiny to burn with fire unquenchable (cf. Mt 3,12; Lc 3,17).

The Padre explained his way of behaviour in the confessional or whenever he needed to rebuke someone to another spiritual daughter, Maria Fusco: "I never sadden anyone but try to always comfort souls if I do reproach someone, it is for the benefit of their soul"[29].

After these examples, which tend to give a justification or explanation to the severity used by Padre Pio in the confessional, I wish to make a personal comment.

Fr. Benedetto Nardella, spiritual director of our Saint, left some notes, " *Appunti su Padre Pio*" which he intended to use to write a biography on Padre Pio. Note n. 35 says: "Padre Pio has experienced the torments of hell in seeing the damned suffer. About two years ago (1919) every 10 or 15 days he underwent this agony. He felt the pains of the senses and of damnation finding himself in body and soul amongst the damned and the demons, in order to save others and himself from that place where they were destined if grace had not helped them[30].

We may not be far from the truth, if we affirm that in front

---

[28]   Rina Giostrelli in Telfener, San Giovanni Rotondo 6.5.1983.

[29]   Testimony written by Maria Fusco.

[30]   R. FABIANO, *Una biografia di Padre Pio incompiuta e il suo autore*, in *Studi su Padre Pio*, anno III – n. 3, September-December 2002, 396.

of sin and of who commits it, Padre Pio, sitting in the confessional was unable not to think about the terrifying consequences that the disobedience of God's laws bring, Hell and
eternal unhappiness. When man's choice to ignore God's laws
becomes a dangerous habit that risks to become unbreakable.
His interventions which could seem to be almost unacceptably
violent sprung from this but in truth it had the energy of the
witness who having suffered unprecedented tortures, wishes
to warn, through whatever measure possible his brothers and
sisters who carelessly walk on the edge of a deep abyss.

His language

Given the large number of people who went to him to
confess, Padre Pio could not spend a long time in clarifying
conversations as he did at the beginning of his priesthood;
therefore he had to adopt the style of the ancient prophets who
sometimes concentrated God's message in a few words. But
what truth shone from those numbered words!

With regards to Padre Pio's way of expressing himself, sister Maria Francesca Foresti of Bologna[31], who died in holiness,

---

[31] Sr. Maria Francesca Foresti was born in Bologna on 17 February 1878
and when Christened was given the name of Eleonora.
On 19 October 1985 she started thinking about consecrating her life to the
Lord. During the month of October in 1919 she met Padre Pio of Pietrelcina and spoke to him about her wish to found a religious institute. The
Saint said he was in favour of this initiative, of her wish to make amends
for insults made to Jesus and for the Franciscan spirit which guided her. He
also helped Miss Foresti to outline the rules and with regards to the vocations he promised he would have prayed. Eleonora stayed in San Giovanni
Rotondo for quite a few days; she returned in February 1920 and then again
in 1921. The rules of the institute were approved by the congregation of

said that Jesus in a vision speaking of Padre Pio said: "His language is gentle, cutting, frank and mysterious like mine: it disheartens, humiliates and provokes with the same austerity because I live in him".

We note the thought of one of his spiritual children about the internal clarity of the Padre's behaviour in the confessional.

"Padre Pio goes straight to the point, to Christ, Crucified Christ. All the obstacles he finds along the way are pushed away, hypocrisies were however thrown, spiritual narcissism unhinged, the incorrect irregular devotions are put right, the gasping religious spirit is revived, the limping Christian spirit is cured, the balance on the edge of sin mortified, the alternatives to Christian commitments torn apart. He is not the Saint of those who regret the hard times of the past but of those who breathe the gentle breeze of the future. He is the Saint who remains stable with, He who was, who is and who ever will be" in He who said "I am".

Charity and severity

The fact that love and harsh methods can go hand in hand in one of God's ministers, when he is zealously inspired to save his brothers, was seen by those who really knew Padre Pio and who had personally proved that sweetness and strength, lashes and caresses can join together, because they come from the same paternal heart full of excellent charity.

the Religious on 26 September 1943. Sr. Maria Francesca Foresti died in Maggio di Oggiano (BO) on 12 November 1953. P. D'Armando, Madre M. Francesca Foresti, Eco Editore, 1287, 7. 110-111.

This is affirmed by masters of the faith and spiritual fathers.

With regards to spiritual charity St. Augustine writes: "When we talk about mutual charity we must be careful not to identify it with pusillanimity or with idle passivity. Being charitable does not mean being weak. Do not think you love your pet only because you don't give it the punishment deserved, or that you love your son, only because you leave him to himself, or that you love your neighbour only because you don't' reprimand him. This is not charity but weakness.

Charity is a force that urges to correct and raise the others. Charity takes delight in good behaviour and tries to amend bad behaviour. Do not love the mistake but the man. If you really love the man you correct him. Even if sometimes you have to be hard, do it for the sake of the greater good of the neighbour"[32].

St. Gregory the Great explained how even disdain in the saints is the result of the righteousness and love, and not of arrogance and contempt of the brothers: "Although even the just usually get angry with sinners...their justice is pitiful . One thing is acting under the impulse of haughtiness, another is for the zeal of discipline and moral principles. The just therefore, are irritated without getting irritated…, they cause persecution, but for the sake of love, as, if for the sake of the discipline outwardly they exaggerate, inwardly charity keeps them in a state of gentleness. In their soul at the first place they put those they correct and repute even better those they judge"[33].

All those who arrive at San Giovanni Rotondo for the first

---

[32] PL 35, 2034.
[33] Homiliae in Evangelia, 2, 34, 2; PL 76.

time remain astonished at the sight of the various pavilions of
the hospital. They cannot help but think about the greatness
of Padre Pio's heart, which managed to give birth to a work
which would bring relief to the suffering of the sick; but to
measure and describe his charity for souls, perhaps no one will
ever have the ability to express it in a few brief words. One
expression however the Padre himself has offered us.

One day in the garden during the evening break, the conversation turned to the love the Saint nourished for sinners. He
pointing to the bulk of the Home for the Relief of Suffering,
which could be seen looking through the cypress trees said: "If
it was necessary to blow it up to save a soul, I wouldn't think
twice about it"[34].

If seeing physical suffering upset him, with regards to moral sickness the Saint wrote. "I suffer greatly, fot not being able
to win all my brothers to God. At certain moments I am on
the point of dying from the pangs my heart endures in seeing
so many suffering souls and my inability to help them and so
many brothers allied with Satan"[35].

3. Padre Pio, charismatic priest and diligent servant

To put Padre Pio's method of confessing in a fixed scheme
is almost impossible. This is because the Padre was a charismatic man who acted, under the influence of the Holy Spirit,
sometimes in an unexplainable way that was amazing and
at others in the same fashion as many other diligent, caring

---

[34]   Testimony of Enzo Bertani, San Giovanni Rotondo 21.2.1995.
[35]   PADRE PIO da PIETRELCINA, *Buona Giornata,* by Fr. Gerardo Di Flumeri,
Ed. Padre Pio da Pietrelcina, San Giovanni Rotondo, 1994, p. 121-122.

confessors that each one of us may have met on our path of faith. One thing however is certain: every one noted the Confession in that Holy Priest was an extra-ordinary event for the soul.

Anna Baroni says: "When we went to his confessional, it was as if were doing an examination, and not only of a particular of our life, but of whole way of being. What joy when we could say: "He gave me absolution!". It was feeling that one was in God's grace"[36].

Once Padre Pio said: "In these cases it is like giving a passport to go or visit Paradise, almost being delivered, a place in Heaven whilst one is still on earth"[37].

Why then he was sometimes "father and doctor" and yet other times a severe "judge", we are not to know: it would be like wishing to enter into God's mystery, in which he moved. All we can do is stick to the facts.

"I had booked to confess to Padre Pio, said the same Anna Baroni, and before me there was a woman who had a handicapped son. When the day arrived for our turn, she went to the confessional before me but as soon as she put her foot inside the area marked by the little gate, you could hear Padre Pio shout: "Go away, get out!".

I stood still. Then I took my place and knelt down waiting for the Saint to finish confessing whoever was at the other side of the confessional. I felt lost, as if crushed against the confessional grate. This is how I felt until the Padre opened the grate and with a gentle voice began the rite of Confession.

He listened to me, and gave me absolution. When I asked him to stay close to me because I was alone, without a father

[36] Anna Baroni, Chiavari (GN), 8.12.1994.
[37] *Marian Month*, day 21.

and a mother, he said: "My soul will always keep you company"[38].

Therefore, as it is written in the Gospel: "One shall be taken and the other left" (Mt 24,40).

a) Some of the principles he followed

From the "*Marian Month*" we note that Fr. Pellegrino, who for years managed the stream of penitents who came to Padre Pio's confessional, is able to point out certain criteria which guided the Saint's behaviour in the confessional. One day he explicitly asked the Padre why he "very often" refused to give absolution.

Padre Pio after correcting "very often" into "when it is the case" clarified: "I believe it is necessary to delay absolution when I notice that the penitent doesn't know what he is doing, (that is he doesn't realise he is a Christian), therefore he:
- forgets the values of Heaven for those on earth.
- is a lover of ease and complete idleness.
- he is lukewarm with regards to evangelic precepts and therefore frightened of carrying them out.
- and finally rebels against the "invitation to convert"[39].

Those who understand well what the Sacrament of Penance is, a moment of conversion, that is a radical change of life, cannot but recognise that the elements indicated by Padre Pio are those that do not allow God's minister to give absolution and that cannot be ignored, neither by the penitent nor by the confessor.

---

[38] Anna Baroni, Chiavari 8.12.1994.
[39] *Marian Month*, day 5.

The Christian who is in the condition, indicated by the Padre, is living in practise in absolute paganism or silent apostasy. From a priest's point of view, giving absolution without making the penitent seriously reflect on the grave state of his soul, and without gaining a strong proposal from him to change his style, means profaning the Sacrament.

That this profaning could take place in the confessional of Padre Pio can be verified by those who lived in San Giovanni Rotondo near the venerable Padre.

It is known that except for rare occasions, it was only possible to speak to the Holy Capuchin by confessing to him. Now, given his well known fame as a worker of miracles, there were those who booked a confession, not to return in God's grace, but most of all to tell him their problems and material needs.

We read in *Mese Mariano* how the Padre expressed his sorrow. "They come to confess themselves with the only purpose of asking me to pray for their illness or for their personal matters. The Confession should not be dishonoured in this way!"[40].

The same sadness was shown by the Padre speaking to Probo Vaccarini from Rimini. "They come here in order that I intercede for their convenience: health, a job, a good marriage, and no one asks me for the true grace which is that to accept with love the misfortunes that the Lord allows day by day[41].

The same Vaccarini gives us another episode both amusing and very significant at the same time, which demonstrates the coherence that guided the Padre in his administration of the

---

[40] *Ibid.*
[41] Probo Vaccarini, S. Martino in Venti (Rimini) 14.5.1998.

Sacrament of Forgiveness.

Probo had become a bit like a travelling salesman, as he himself said, between San Giovanni Rotondo and Rimini, and friends and people he knew often loaded him up with messages and things to do for them when he was planning to leave for San Giovanni Rotondo. He said: "Once in order not to cut a poor figure, I wrote on a piece of paper a long list of things to ask the Padre. Eight people wanted things doing.

Whilst I was confessing, my thoughts were turned more to when it would be the right moment to ask my holy confessor these favours, than to the Sacrament. Padre Pio who missed nothing noticed my lack of spiritual concentration and became grumpy. He asked me some rapid questions, absolved me and brusquely dismissed me. "Off you go lad".

I hadn't even had time to open my list and stammered: "Father, but what shall I say to my friends?".

The Padre didn't change his mood and severely said: "Is this how you confess? Either you go away now, or I will". And he stood up.

I was full of anguish and couldn't move. The Padre understood how uncomfortable I felt and sat down more gently saying: "All right, get on with it".

I looked at my note, I turned it over and over in my hands, but it was always white. There was nothing written on it. "Come on lad, get on with it. There are others waiting", he repeated.

I tried once more to read but the note was always blank. At the same time I saw the Padre smiling. Helpless I said: "Father, I don't understand anything any more".

Then he said: "Keep calm" and he gave me seven answers, one after the other, but not the eight because the petitioner had the time and means to go to San Giovanni Rotondo and personally speak to Padre Pio[42].

Padre Pio during a Confession always acted in a correct perfect way. "I administer Christ's blood", he said to Fr. Carmelo of Sessano, the Superior of the friary.

Fr. Giovanni Sammarone, one of our confrères who lived in San Giovanni Rotondo, states that the Saint was "precis" when confessing, and added: "Sometimes, when I was confessing and I didn't follow his line of thoughts he used to say: " Well lad, if you want to go to hell, I don't. You want to pull me there too"[43].

---

[42] This episode heard from the voice of the witness on 14.5.1998, can also be read in his book *Colloqui con Padre Pio*, Ed. La Casa Sollievo della Sofferenza, San Giovanni Rotondo 1996, 55. It is worth giving a profile of this spiritual son to see how his life developed in the hands of Providence. Probo Vaccarini was born in Rimini in 1919. The area of Arco Augusto was where he spent the carefree days of his youth. Soon after getting a job on the Railway, he was called up to arms and left for Russia. Despite the terrible atrocities he managed to get home in time to assist his dying mother. After improving his economical and social position (becoming a surveyor) he had a spiritual crisis. Taking a friend's advice he met Padre Pio. This meeting marked him for the rest of his life. When he was 33 year old he married Anna Maria Vannuchi. They had four sons and three daughters. Three of the sons became priests. After his wife's death Probo became first acolyte and the deacon of a church in Rimini. His experience in the parish of San Martino in Venti, in the outskirts of Rimini, gave him the push to carry out an old dream. On 8 May 1988 Mgrs. Giovanni Locatelli ordained him presbyter. Now he is the parish priest of San Martino in Venti." PROBO VACCARINI, *Anch'io..., pendolare del Padre*.

[43] Fr. Giovanni Sammarone from Triveneto, lived in San Giovanni Rotondo from 9.9.1948 until 13.1.1951. He was the friary's cook. His testimony was given in Larino on 9.9. 1986.

The pain caused by sins

The Padre defined Confession "a rebirth, living again using one's reason and crying for one's mistakes"[44].

"Crying for one's mistakes" is nothing other than living in the state of mind which the Catechism of the Catholic Church calls contrition, that is, "the pain of the soul and the reprobation of the sin committed, followed by the purpose not to sin again in the future"(n. 1451). This is the first thing the penitent must do to return to a state of grace.

The saints showed their pain and disapproval of sin in a sensitive way, with tears as did Peter when he caught our Lord's eye after denying Him (Lc 22-62) and they worked a s perfectly as hey could in fear and trepidation, never feeling completely faultless.

Dr. Franco Lotti told us that one day he found Padre Pio in his room crying. He asked the Saint why he was shedding those tears and was answered: "I am crying at the thought of when I will have to be in God's presence".

He tried to comfort his spiritual father, saying he was completely hat God would not have found any real faults with him on Judgement Day.

Padre Pio who had the shutters of his window half-closed, and was in the semi-darkness put the light on and said: "You didn't see the dust on this table, but now you can notice it. And explaining once more his tears: "Do you understand I am not worried about the faults that I know, but about those He will put before me. If I am at fault I will fall to my knees and He will forgive me. But for those I don't know, will he give me the time to kneel down before condemning me?" And he

---

[44] *Marian Month*, day 5.

continued to sob in front of his spiritual son who was very embarrassed.[45]

Many know Padre Pio as a confessor, but few know that he, a penitent himself took great care of the cleanliness of his own soul and often went to Confession. He scrupulously examined his faults and shortcoming with great humility.

Fr. Pellegrino says: "Whilst preparing himself for Confession, he invoked Our Lady and wept. To be honest he cried so many tears that with these alone, in my opinion he could have cancelled all his sins and those of the others".

Once I said to him that before Confession he carried out a kind of "sacramental rite" made with prayers to Our Lady and the "holy water" of his tears. He realised that I had ears dropped at his door and heard his ejaculations and cries, and he said: "So now to cry for my sins I need to ask your permission, do I?".

In another occasion, always referring to Confession, I said to him that he was like a child who as soon as he dirtied a finger, ran to his mum to have it cleaned.

"That is so" he said and that is what I wish to do. You are better than me, you can purify yourself and do without a confessor. With God's help I hope I will never believe that I am self-sufficient"[46].

The recount by Fr. Pellegrino, who shows us how carefully Padre Pio prepared his Confession and his yearning for abso-

---

[45] Franco Lotti, from Bologna, was head-physician of paediatrics for many years at the hospital "Home for the Relief of Suffering". When he was very young he met Padre Pio and he stayed near him, moving to the Gargano. We listened to his testimony on 19.9.1987 in San Giovanni Rotondo.
[46] This testimony is taken from the deposition made by the confrère during Padre Pio's Beatification process; see pp. 23-24.

lute purity, is followed by that of Fr. Eusebio Notte who shows us how the Saint lived every sacrament intimately.

One day Padre Pio asked the young confrère to listen to his Sacramental Confession. When he had finished confessing his sins, he burst into tears. Fr Eusebio was surprised and said: "But Father, I can't see any proportion between the sins you have confessed and your display of such pain and sorrow".

And the Padre replied: "My son, sin is not only breaking God's laws. No! Most of all sin is betraying love. "Do you know how many gifts the Lord has given me? And have I answered Him? I am the biggest sinner on this earth!" And he continued to cry sorrowfully[47].

Padre Pio didn't expect the penitents who came to him to return in God's Grace, to show their sorrow through tears, he desired that they would have expressed their desire to change their way of life and really convert. Those who were not ready to take the road of improvement and perfection found him to be completely against them like an insurmountable wall, when they expected to be absolved.

We have already mentioned a discussion which took place during a break when the Padre defended his "intransigence" with some penitents who showed no sign of amendment.[48] But there is something more to add. One of those present commented: "Father, but sometimes one suffers painfully for his sins and you refuse to absolve him just the same".

---

[47] Fr. Eusebio Notte lived with Padre Pio during the last years of his Holy life and precisely from October 1960 to May 1965, looking after him lovingly during the day, and when the Padre was in need, also during the night. His testimony was given in Morcone on 17.8.1994.

[48] See pp. 23-24.

And Padre Pio: "Pain, pain!...Pain is measured by the actions which come after. When one comes with the same sin a second, third and fourth time, what pain has it got? The confessor is at the same time father, judge and doctor; yes, even a doctor and there are evils – and he turned to the doctors who were present that one can't feel, that are not noted even by those who are in deep water. One deludes himself he is well whilst he is completely done for"[49].

Let us see some examples of how the Padre administered the Sacrament of Forgiveness.

1. Umberto Antonelli from Marcianise (CE) between 1954 and 1955 came to San Giovanni Rotondo and confessed to Padre Pio. When he finished telling his sins the Padre asked him: "Is there anything else?" and he replied no.

The Padre repeated the question and once more he replied no. For the third time the Saint asked "Anything else?".

At this third denial there was an uproar. "He", said the penitent "with a voice that was not his, but that of the Holy Spirit shouted: "Get out, get out, because you are still not sorry for your sins!".

I remained petrified, also because I felt ashamed in front of so many people. I tried to say something but he pressed on: "Be quiet, you chatterbox, you've said enough. Now I wish to speak. Isn't it true that you go to dancehalls?".

When I answered yes he said: "And don't you know that dancing is an invitation to sin?".

Astonished I didn't know what to say: in my wallet I had the membership card for a dancehall, of which I hadn't thought about in the least. I promised to mend my ways and after a

---

[49] *Chronicle…*, 17th December 1957.

while he gave me absolution".[50]

2. Biagio Fusco, from San Martino in Pensilis (CB), went to San Giovanni Rotondo to meet Padre Pio whom his wife had spoken to him about. During his Confession he was struck by the fact that Padre read his soul with God's light.

A few years later he returned again to confess but whist he was saying his sins he heard his confessor shout at him: "You are a relapsed sinner!" He finally understood what kind of conversion the Saint demanded. Therefore, having promised to mend his ways, he started to follow God's path under such a sure and demanding guidance.

The Padre took him amongst his spiritual children. Biagio was also privileged to receive a letter from the Padre who encouraged him to confide in God's goodness and forgiveness[51].

3. M. G. says: "In 1963 I was encouraged by Paolo Sartori, who accompanied me, to go and confess to Padre Pio. He didn't even let me kneel down, assailing me with a flood of words of fire; the cleanest expression being that of "filthy person". I thought I would die of shame.

As only God knows I went away from the confessional and, after coming out of a state of shock I went to another priest who said: "If Padre Pio treated you like that it means he cares about you. He wants to save you". And after listening to me patiently he pronounced the following sentence: "You must change your ways!".

---

[50]   Umberto Antonelli, San Giovanni Rotondo, May 1993.

[51]   Cf. PADRE PIO OF PIETRELCINA, *Epistolario IV, Corrispondenza con diverse categorie di persone*, edited by Melchiorre da Pobladura and Alessandro da Ripabottoni, Ed. "Padre Pio da Pietrelcina", San Giovanni Rotondo, 2002, 625-626.

My faith was superficial, I believed I could save my soul by saying my night prayers and making the sign of the cross in the morning. I did go to Confession but continued to sin. I betrayed my family and I didn't always act honestly in the business I ran. After meeting the Padre, something started to change: bit by bit I discovered my biggest sin was that of not repenting.

I continued to go to San Giovanni Rotondo to see the Padre, I counted a first, a second and up to seven visits at a distance of a few months one from the other, but I kept well away from his confessional.

Once I went to the San Francesco Hall, where the Padre usually went after the women's confession, but stayed in a corner, just to see him pass by. When he came out of the lift I turned my head and followed him with the corner of my eye. The little crowd of people divided to make space for him: he folded his arms across his chest and didn't let anybody kiss his hands. Instead he came towards me and stretched out his hand. I kissed it and he blessed me. I started to feel more courageous.

One day I gathered my strength together. As I had booked I neared the confessional and the first thing I said was : "Father, I repent , I meant to say: I grieve, because I do not repent my sins".

"And is this not repentance?", said the Saint to my great relief. Then he let me tell him my sins and gave me absolution. When I left the confessional I felt as though I was flying"[52].

---

[52] Thiene 2.5.1996.

The accusation of sins

Another essential element for the Sacrament of Forgiveness, that the Padre called for to make the Sacrament complete, was the accusation of the faults committed. The Catechism of the Catholic Church reminds us that by accusing himself "man looks in the face the sins he has committed and takes upon responsibility for them" (n. 1455).

A spiritual son offers us a precious testimony with Padre Pio's intention to face the penitent with the moral law that had been violated.

"In front of Padre Pio", he said, "one was an open book, which he could read from at his pleasure". Sometimes in Confession I was so nervous that I couldn't say a word. The Padre waited patiently. So I to get out of difficulty used to say: "Father, you know all".

He replied: "I know that I know, but it is you who must tell me all in which you have sinned"[53].

Naturally the accusation the Holy confessor expected had to be clear and detailed, especially for grave faults: in this he followed the Church laws. The Catechism states: "During confession the penitents must list all the deadly sins, they are aware of after a scrupulous examination of conscience" (n. 1456).

Testimonies and experience tell us that the Padre was neither over-meticulous nor inflexible and tried in all ways to help the penitent to see clearly the state of his soul, by asking questions. But he would not accept imprecise answers.

---

[53]   Ippolito Nievo, form Florence, one of the spiritual children we will find again in his book as a witness, told us this in San Giovanni Rotondo on 27 September 1994.

1. To a scrupulous priest Padre Pio once asked: "Have you told lies?".

Feeling under examination, the penitent became uncertain and answered: "Perhaps".

And the Padre: "Have you or haven't you? If you haven't why are you saying perhaps?[54].

2. The questions of God's diligent minister were to do with what kind of sin had been committed and how many times. Padre Pio asked them to complete the examination of conscience that the diligent penitent should have carried out carefully and to which he always used to call attention.

To Mario Sanci, who in 1946 went to the confessional more to ask for a "look" at his body instead of his soul he asked the usual question: "How long is it since your last Confession?".

"I don't remember", he said, showing a complete lack of preparation for Confession.

The Saint Confessor remained silent for a while and then continued: "Do you go to church?".

"I've missed ten or twenty times".

Padre Pio: "*Lad*, after ten comes eleven not twenty. Go away".

"Can I come back?", asked the penitent.

"Yes, but you must make a good examination of conscience", replied the Padre[55].

3. In asking for the precise number of serious sins, the Saint gave the penitent the moral reasons for his strictness. B. P.

54   Don Bruno Borelli, Erba (CO) 2.11.1996.
55   Mario Sanci, Salemi (TR) 2.11.1996.

confessed saying he had had bad thought against chastity; the Padre asked: "How many times?".

He answered: "Six or seven".

To which the diligent Confessor replied: "Seven is not the same as six, because it means one more deadly sin".

As the penitent was unable to give the precise number of the transgressions, Padre Pio sent him away[56].

4. Mrs P. P. offers us the testimonies of three Confessions she had had with the Padre. During the first in 1956 she said: "I have doubted my faith".

Padre Pio: "How many times?".

"Infinitely", answered the penitent.

At this vague and general answer the Padre rebuked: Only God is infinitely". And he closed the grate.

The next time she tried to be more precise admitting the same sin.

"How many times?", asked Padre Pio.

"Ten times", she replied.

"You have sold your soul to the devil ten times. This time the Padre put the stress on the danger of wandering for a long time in darkness; where the evil spirit can undermine the certainties of the faith, bit by bit until the soul no longer believes.

The woman, she herself admits, had no knowledge about confession and pointed out to Padre Pio: "This is the second time that you send me away."

And the Saint: "Who goodness knows how many more times you will be sent away".

The penitent went for the third time and this time the Padre greeted her with gentleness, helping her to examine her con-

---

[56]   San Giovanni Rotondo 4.10.1994.

science. "I want to help you", he said. Then he began to ask: "Have you done this? Did you do that?". And she answered either yes or no.

The woman ended by saying: "In this way the Padre let me understand a little at the time what the sacrament was really about, he absolved me and let me go in peace"[57].

We add that P. P. became one of those spiritual daughters that in order to live near the Padre, moved to San Giovanni Rotondo.

These interventions, that sometimes seem at the end of insensitivity and rudeness, were part of a long mysterious selection and preparation, reserved in a special way to those souls who would have become part of his big family.

The reasons behind his questions and the value of his words

Sometimes the Padre through his questions gave the clear impression that, more than looking for light for himself, he wished to make the penitents fully aware of the state of their souls.

1. Anna Baroni says: "During Confession the Padre was very precise, he wanted to get the truth. Once, about something I had mentioned , he asked: "Why?".

I answered a few words but he was not satisfied and repeated : "Why?".

I added something else.

And he for the third time said: "Why?".

I added an insignificant detail. Until seeing me in a state of

---

57   San Giovanni Rotondo 6.5.1995.

confusion, he found the way to make things clear within my soul"[58].

2. Eolo Soldaini too underlines the importance of the brief but precious conversations with Padre Pio. Born on 23 May 1914 in Livorno, Eolo was a navy officer and after many positions in various naval towns of Europe, he was offered a very advantageous job in Australia. Not knowing if he should accept the job or not, between 1956-57 he went to Padre Pio and he prepared for the Confession he was to make a few days after his arrival.

After confessing the first sin he paused, then he got stuck. Padre Pio intervened: "Since your last Confession you haven't done this, this and this. Eolo heard him list four sins.

At the Padre's words he had and extraordinary inner illumination of both mind and heart. "I saw the unknown", he says. He realised what it meant to live the faith, live the life of the spirit; at the same time he felt a distancing from earthly things. Then he felt a mysterious voice from within which clearly said: "You must not go to Australia, because serious family problems would drive you to desperation: you would have to throw yourself in the sea".

After receiving absolution he returned home and decided to stay in Italy.

After six or seven months those "serious problems" predicted from above came to be. Being in the homeland and working serenely helped find a remedy where it was all possible. Knowing what he had done all that was humanely possible to bring peace and serenity.

He confesses: "In those few minutes near to the Padre I had three miracles: Padre Pio read my heart, he illuminated me

---

[58]   Anna Barone, Chiavari 27.9.1995.

with regards to spiritual life, and he gave me the answer to my future"[59].

3. Sr. Elia Centrone tells us:

"We sisters who worked in the hospital Home for the Relief of Suffering, had Fr. Clemente from Postiglione as our ordinary confessor. I noticed that other young nuns like myself, had long conversations whist I stayed in the confessional just a few minutes. After scrupulously telling my sins and an admonishment or two from that Holy Man, my Confession ended.

Every so often, it was our turn to go to Padre Pio who acted as an extra-ordinary confessor. One day I explained to Padre Pio my doubt that I didn't know how to confess properly or open my heart to my spiritual father. He said: "Do you declare all your sins with the intention not to commit them again?".

I answered: "I surely do Father".

And the Saint: "Well then you are right: this is the essence of Confession".

But with Padre Pio it was completely different; he wanted to know everything even little things"[60].

4. Dr. Gusso, a spiritual son of Padre Pio and for many years sanitary director of the Home for the Relief of Suffering, says: "When Padre Pio gave advice his words were clear, balanced and easily understandable. His answers with regards to moral problems left no doubts. Even when he was out of confession he was always bright: he enjoyed a joke and always had an answer"[61].

---

[59] Eolo Soldaini, Taranto, 31.5.1999.

[60] Sr. Elia Centrone, Conversano 20.6.1996

[61] Dr. Giuseppe Gusso, One of the main figures in the Home for the Relief of Suffering; San Giovanni Rotondo 12.11.1994.

5. We end with a statement from Pina Patti: "Padre Pio's way of confessing was always new and very particular. When he saw commitment and effort he encouraged; for some persistent faults he said: "Thank the Lord that he keeps you in holy humbleness". Or: "There are certain faults that we will even take to heaven". When we were deeply sorry for our mistakes he treated us with motherly kindness: instead if he thought we were stuck to sin, he treated us badly"[62].

b) A particular pain of the Holy Confessor

We have seen how sometimes the Padre was forced to send the penitent away because he hadn't the right disposition to be absolved. However this pained the Padre greatly. From *Marian Month* we can see that in these occasions the first one to be punished was himself, Padre Pio. With humility and responsibility he explained to Fr. Pellegrino: "When I don't give absolution, it is to myself that I don't give it"[63].

With this the Saint wanted to say he felt he hadn't done all that was necessary in order that the penitent could deserve God's forgiveness: that is he had not prayed enough, he hadn't suffered and paid enough.

This was the real drama that the venerable Padre lived deep inside himself when he refused absolution to someone: in confession he judged himself first and then the others!

---

[62] Pina Patti, San Giovanni Rotondo 6.5.1995.
[63] *Marian Month*, day 21.

The sick at his confessional

It is known how sensitive Padre Pio was towards the people in difficulty who he met in his daily life, when going amongst them every morning and afternoon to hear them in Confession he suffered for their afflictions and worries. But if alongside moral sufferings there was physical suffering it seemed as if his heart would break.

How many times those who helped or kept him company noticed that, when he saw a body in pain, especially if it was a child who was suffering, his features changed. A shadow spread over the luminous divine reflexes of his face and in his countenance contracted in a painful but composed spasm, as if the suffering of the sick child entered his flesh.

Fr Pellegrino notes: "Deep sentiments of compassion flowed in his soul when he met the sick especially if they were children. Sometimes he seemed almost paralysed and could do nothing more than cry for them. Once in fact he said "Oh, if only I could destroy all the pain on this earth! But he quickly corrected himself saying: "And who am I who wishes to do that which God does not do?"[64].

We know what he said of the suffering: "In every man there is Jesus, but in the sick we can see Jesus twice". In that case charity and love became an obligation for the Saint .

Don Pasquale Cantalupo, in one of our meetings spoke of his joy in having known and confessed to Padre Pio. "I was ill and the Padre at the end of the Confession comforted me and let me go.

---

[64] PADRE PIO DA PIETRELCINA, *Testimonianze*, edited by P. Vincenzo (Frezza) da Casacalenda. Ed. "Padre Pio da Pietrelcina", Friary S. Giovanni Rotondo (FG) 1970, 114.

Whilst I was leaving the confessional I stopped and asked: "Father, but aren't you going to give me a penance?".

And Padre Pio answered: "haven't you already got enough? Do you want more?"[65].

Alongside this love for the suffering the Saint added also that for those who assisted and looked after the sick.

Maria Teresa Brevi tells us: "My mother confessed to Padre Pio who after she had confessed her faults said: "I will not give you any penance as you have already done it. Your sins are remitted because for 23 years you have been looking after your husband who is in a wheelchair. You have had a long hard road, but you will have a tranquil peaceful death".

The words of Padre Pio came true. My mother had a heart attack at 15.30. The priest was called to give her the extreme unction. She died at 20.30.

Before she passed away, she said to her five children who gathered round her bed: "Love the two twins". These were the children of a neighbour she had looked after at our house for 14 years"[66].

A particularly difficult moment for the Padre was when he saw critically ill people kneeling at his feet, who did not have the necessary inclination to make a good Confession and who had only gone to him to recover their physical health: "These are the moments when I would like to run away, to disappear from the face of the earth, because I, I become the cause of their eventual deception with regards to the condition of their spirit"[67]. The Padre could not break the rules he followed to

---

[65]   Don Pasquale Cantalupo, Conversano 30.10.1999.

[66]   M. Teresa Brevi, San Giovanni Rotondo 7.10.2004.

[67]   *Marian Month*, day 5.

administer the Sacrament. Even for the sick there was the expression "go away!".

The Padre's discomfort can be seen reading what he wrote to his spiritual father Fr. Benedetto:

"When I know that a person is afflicted in soul or body, what would I not do to have the Lord relieve him of his sufferings! Willingly would I take upon myself all his afflictions in order to see him saved, and I would even hand over to him the benefits of such sufferings if the Lord would allow it".

And in closing the letter the Saint added a detail which throws a bright light on the nature of that tenderness he felt for his fellowmen: "I clearly quite clearly that this is a most singular favour from God"[68].

So he found himself trapped between his compassion for the sick person and his duty to "worthily administer the blood of Christ". And he was forced to admit: "They like the others, like everyone must understand that Confession is a rebirth, a fresh way of living, crying for all their mistakes"[69].

Naturally, people seeing a sick person brusquely and quickly sent away from the confessional, easily thought about the humiliation suffered by the penitent rather than what happened in the minister of God's heart, plus they could have no idea of the reason behind the refusal of absolution.

In June 1950 a prayer group from Biella, one of the first born in Italy, organised a pilgrimage to San Giovanni Rotondo.

---

[68] Letters I, 519: 26.3.1914.
[69] *Marian Month*, day 5.

At Milan, another group from Como and surrounding towns joined the 23 pilgrims on the train. Amongst these was a 27 year old handsome young man who due to a misfortune was blind and had become sceptic and almost non-believer.

On the 14th they reached their destination and they all booked to confess to Padre Pio. Even the poor blind joined the queue; but when he knelt down he was sent away by the Padre. His dismay was felt by the entire group.

Together they prayed for him. He was encouraged to try again, but the second attempt went badly too. At last after a few days the saint absolved him; and not only but also said: "I'll see you again in a month's time".

So, reconciled with God and himself, the young man left happily with the other pilgrims, and told them that with the help of the Padre he had willingly renounced at the light of his eyes to have the light of his soul[70].

But the testimony which is richer in touching details is that given to us by Graziano Borelli.

"One day a desperate mother came to me asking for help. Knowing that I often went to San Giovanni Rotondo, she asked me to accompany her, her husband and their 14 year old son, who was suffering with a lymphogranuloma of the neck, to see Padre Pio and ask for his intercession and obtain a miracle from God, only that could have saved her son.

I accepted, rather worried about the responsibility I was taking on and we left to go to the Padre.

When we arrived I was trying to find for the right moment to speak to him when luckily Bro. Gioavanni Sammarone came to my help, letting me enter cell number 1, after the Saint had

---

[70] From documents provided by Carla Mancia, prayer group leader from Biella: 7 December 1999.

returned from hi meeting with the people.

"Father, I have brought a 14 year old boy who is ill with a lymphogranuloma", I began.

"And what can I do about it?" answered Padre Pio.

"Father, if you pray, God can make a miracle".

"Do you believe what you say?".

"Yes Father, I do believe it".

He remained in silence for a while and added: "So let it be!".

I was sure in my heart that the boy would have been cured. In the meantime, waiting outside was the boy's father. As he was sceptical and not close to God, I wanted the Padre to say something to him. So as I went out instead of pulling the door closed I made him welcome in. When the Padre saw him he sent him out without a second thought.

The man came out and when he arrived in the square, he started to shout abuse: "Where have you brought me? That fellow is not a saint, he certainly isn't a saint! I tried to calm him down without success. As I had booked a Confession with the Padre for me, the boy and his father, I thought to myself: "now when it's his turn to confess he'll get the rest". He hadn't taken part in the Sacraments for years.

After waiting a few days our turn arrived.

The boy's father entered for first, behind the curtain where Padre Pio confessed. From my place I heard the Padre grumbling and protesting; and I feared the worst that he would have been thrown out. Instead I saw my friend come out looking serene.

Then the son, the sick boy went in: the Padre didn't absolve him and sent him away.

The father who a little while before had calmed down, became upset once more. He could not understand why Padre

Pio, even though he had given him a good shaking down after being away from the Church for so many years, had absolved him and yet at poor sick boy he had refused absolution.

I didn't know what to say to calm him down.

We left. We stopped at Loreto, the shrine dear to Padre Pio and run by Capuchin Friars. Heaven helped us, because we met a friar who ignoring the other pilgrims dedicated his attention to us. He took the sick boy to one side, helped him make a good confession and so we could all take communion together.

We stopped again at Collevalenza, where we had the chance to see Mother Speranza and to speak about the problem that had caused us to make that journey. She said to us: "If that Holy Man of San Giovanni Rotondo answered your plea saying "So be it", you have already obtained the grace".

When they returned to Pistoia, the mother took the sick boy to hospital for a check-up. The doctors were amazed by the improvement in his condition. They didn't give a final judgement but delayed the diagnosis to a later day after other check ups.

Unfortunately the father who had completely taken in heart, one day returning form the hospital where he had gone to collect his son, was knocked down by a car and died instantly. He was unable to enjoy seeing his son perfectly cured.

However, Padre Pio at San Giovanni Rotondo had put him back in God's Grace ready to meet him. The boy was completely cured and is still living today, as a good Christian after the Padre's lesson[71].

---

[71]   Graziano Borelli, Pistoia, 9.10.1999.

The confessor becomes a doctor

The Padre, far from being insensitive to the every day problems of his penitents, at the end of a Confession always allowed everyone to tell him about the difficulties they had to face. He patiently listened, gave advice and comfort. He didn't hurry thinking of the people who were waiting, or do anything else that could make the person he was talking to feel uncomfortable. In this way those who spoke had the clear impression that Padre Pio was at their complete disposal, as if at that moment for that Saint Confessor there was only himself and the penitent kneeling at his feet.

But it is to be underlined that often it was the confessional that was the privileged place where the Lord carried out healing, through Padre Pio's faithful servant.

1. Paolo Perrone came from Sicily to San Giovanni Rotondo in December 1948. After confessing he said he was worried because he thought he had pleurisy, having a constant pain in the shoulder. Padre Pio listened and said: "And do you want to live with this worrying thought my son? Put your faith in God. Look, I have rotten lungs and yet I'm still living".

And after a pause, he put his hand on the man's shoulder and he said: "Besides, does it hurt you now?". The man waited a while before answering, because he couldn't have any doubt about his constant pain.

The Padre repeated the question: "But does it hurt or not?".

And Perrone, after a minute's hesitation, examining himself carefully had to admit that in that moment he felt no pain whatsoever. So the Padre said: "There have you seen??!". And the penitent returned home cured[72].

---

[72] Paolo Perrone, San Giovanni Rotondo 30.4.1993.

2. Danilo Gonin, in the fifties, returned to Italy from Canada, because he was suffering with a throat tumour. "Go to your homeland to die, because nothing can be done for you" the doctors had told him straight forwardly.

When he arrived home he told his wife everything and she immediately suggested a trip to San Giovanni Rotondo. Here, after waiting a few days, Danilo could kneel down in Padre Pio's confessional.

As soon as he saw him he said: "Eh, Canadian!".

The sick man was so surprised he couldn't say a word and he burst into tears. Padre Pio after comforting him told him to go away for a moment, to calm down and let the others who were waiting go ahead.

The following day he returned and confessed. The Padre after giving absolution, before the man made a single hint about his problem, asked: "So what do the doctors say about your illness?".

When the penitent answered that the most optimistic doctor hadn't given him more than three months to live, the Saint touching his swollen throat said: "Have faith, Jesus is doctor and medicine".

Whilst the man was returning by car to Vicenza, when he got near Loreto, he realised he was breathing without any difficulty.

Once he arrived home went for new medical examinations; but he was found to be completely healthy and had no further problems[73].

3. Umbero Di Girolamo from Palermo had been sick for five years, first with a recurring intestinal infection, then with

---

[73]   Danilo Golin, Tiene 6.5.1996.

polisierosite; then with exudative peritonitis and pleurisy first on the right side then on the left then on the right again. To all this was added Poth's disease. He had worn a plaster cast for five months, a second for another six and another for seven months.

During this last period in the winter of 1955 he came to San Giovanni Rotondo. It snowed for four consecutive days, so much it was impossible to leave the boarding house. He had decided he might as well go back to Palermo, but Mrs Lotti, the mother of Dr. Franco Lotti persuaded him to stay.

On the fifth day he finally went up to the Friary. He went into the sacristy and found a large group of men, but a space opened and he saw two friars, a young one who gave a kiss to an older one. He was struck, attracted, magnetized by the eyes of the latter who looked at him closely. He realised he was in front of the Holy man whom they had spoken of.

He would have liked to say something about his state of health, instead he remained dumb. But Padre Pio said: "Lad, but have you got any faith?". As before not a single word left his lips.

Receiving no answer the Saint added: "Well, if it's like that, away with you". Whilst saying this he gave two taps with the back of his hand to the plaster cast on the left side of the chest: "What pain", Umberto said "the Padre must have felt in doing that as his sore hand struck a leather strap of the cast!",

The poor invalid went away upset and agitated into a corner of the sacristy. Later the young priest who had been at Padre Pio's side, Giambattista Calavita, saw him lost and alone and he approached him. "You don't dare saints, but if I were you I would. Don't go away".

"What should I do?" asked Umberto.

"Go back to him and confess".

Di Girolamo booked a Confession and a few days later he

was kneeling at Padre Pio's feet. "How long is it since your last Confession?", asked the Padre.

Once more the words died on the young man's lips. And the Padre: "Away with you".

He went to the boarding house and cried for 3 days and nights but stayed in San Giovanni Rotondo and began to live the life of prayer that took place at the Friary. In the morning he listened to the Padre's 4.45 Mass and in the evening he recited the rosary taking part in the Mass. He went back to the boarding house only to eat and sleep.

One day as the Padre passed by, he looked at him and with a gentle tone said: "Sicilian, Sicilian! What does this Sicilian want?!".

Umberto had an injection of faith. He had become friendly with a good priest, Fr. Clemente form Postiglione, and he had been to confess to him several times.

He finally made his Confession to the Padre with a certain tranquillity.

He received absolution and before leaving he made a sign towards his chest and with his knuckles knocked on his plaster cast. Padre Pio asked: "what have you had?". Umberto answered only: "I've ..." and didn't continue.

Once more the Saint said: "What have you had?" "Father", said the other without going on.

Padre Pio for the third time: "But my son, what have you had?".

Finally the poor man said: "Father, must I offer my sufferings to Our Lady?", thinking that perhaps for him there would never be any cure. And the Padre: "We all have the duty to take care of ourselves".

Umberto added: "Father, a lady spoke to me about spiritual children...". But he didn't dare to ask to become one of them and

Padre Pio admitted him to his large family: "Yes sir, yes sir".

The conversation was over.

The young man returned to the guesthouse, but from that day he stopped taking medicines. He stayed in san Giovanni Rotondo for a few months between that Winter and the following Spring.

He returned to Palermo. One day he said to his mother: "The plaster cast is irritating me. I'm going to take it off". His mother didn't know what to answer. And he took it off. He then went to the doctor who found him regenerated, reinvigorated and much better. Without his corset, without medicine, he started to practise sports again.

One day Padre Pio saw Umberto worried about his future and he said to him: "If anything happens to you, I'll be a father to you"[74].

With regards to the cures that the Lord worked through Padre Pio, we must note that in them there was more than anything else a spiritual message.

St. Leone Magno writes that Jesus cured bodies, so that men, "stimulated by material benefits and visible miracles "would be attracted to and confirmed "to his doctrine bearer of salvation": the Lord in this way changed the external cures into interior remedies"[75].

c) An encounter with the Spirit

The Confession with Padre Pio couldn't last long: a few

---

[74]   Umberto Di Girolamo form Palermo, Trapani 28.10.1996.
[75]   Disc. 95, 1,2; PL 54, 461.

minutes, except for rare exceptions, was all everyone had to tell him their problems. More than that was not possible. Too many people were pressing to go to that confessional.

So the Holy Spirit, that encouraged many of God's children who needed graces to come to the Gargano, needed to give this faithful servant some of his gifts, that of clairvoyance and being able to read hearts, to enable him to enter prodigiously into the mystery of the consciences and enlighten them. These charisms were the most authentic credentials that God produced to train him for his pastoral actions.

A phenomena that surprised the penitent was that the Padre could completely know the situation of one's soul with regards to the present and also to the distant past.

One day, Fr. Pasquale Cattaneo told the Saint his worry for a persistent difficulty in his spiritual life. Padre Pio at his first words looked at him and with a harsh tone said: "Still?!".

The good priest went stone cold. It was years that, even though he often confessed to the Padre, he hadn't spoken about that problem; one he had discussed with him a very long time before[76].

We have another testimony that shows how the past, owing to his charism, was perfectly known to the Padre.

Adriana Pallotti says: "There was a time in which my father often came down from Modena to San Giovanni Rotondo to confess to Padre Pio. One of the things he insistently asked for was an increase of faith.

He was absent then for a long time. After three or four years he confessed once more. "Father, I poured out my troubles to a friend, speaking badly about a tenant whom I had allowed

---

[76] Don Pasquale Cattaneo, Fiera di Primiero (TN) 31.7.1988.

to use a little piece of my land. He planted two little trees there but when he moved house he took them away, uprooting them".

And the Saint brusquely and dryly: "And then you ask me to increase your faith?"[77].

We wish now to speak of the sins Padre Pio guessed with the illumination of the Holy Spirit in the confessional.

1. Sr. Pura Pagani, who died in holiness, in San Zeno di Mozzecane (VR) on 2nd July 2001, gives us an example of the Paraclete working in the Saint.

This noble soul said: "I went to Padre Pio's confessional well prepared after a careful examination of my conscience but the Padre, after making the sign of the cross, with which he began the sacramental conversation, anticipated my sins as if he could read them in my heart. He also assured me that I would have received graces which afterwards I really have obtained"[78].

2. However diligence and good will don't always manage to make clear one's interior intrigue. So the Saint intervened with suggestions that came right from on high.

Mrs Raffaella Massidda, who lived a life of scruples and anxiety, the first time she confessed to the Padre in the forties, carefully prepared the sins she had to confess but the Padre interrupted her. "Be quiet, I know what I have to say to you", then added, "Throw all your worries to God. Trust in Him. Let Him take care of you"[79].

---

[77] Adriana Pallotti, San Giovanni Rotondo 5.12.1995.
[78] Sr. Pura Pagani, Mozzecane (VR) 10.5.1997.
[79] Raffaella Massidda, Campobasso 16.4.1991.

3. A chemist from Urbino, S.E., also had a similar experience.

He had come down to San Giovanni Rotondo in 1947, to go to confess to Padre Pio, but people hadn't advised him to be precise and quick when confessing his sins and when he was at the Saint's feet, he tried to read in one breath all he had written.

At a certain point the Padre interrupted the long litany saying: "Shut up chatterbox. What you should say is that you often get angry. Isn't that right, that you soon get angry?".

"Yes father", admitted the penitent.

"Well, then be careful of rage, because all your sins come from this"[80].

4. A nun, who was a nurse in a hospital, had a soft spot for a doctor: Nothing serious, but the voice of her conscience wouldn't leave her in peace. She though about Padre Pio, the only person who could clear the state of her soul.

At last she had the chance to confess to him. She started to say her sins but took time before saying the problem that was troubling her.

The Padre interrupted the delay and thundered: "When are you going to tell me the rest?".

After the initial hesitancy she explained all her state of mind. "Go, and find a confessor. I'm not giving you absolution", was the answer with which he ended the conversation[81].

5. Luciano Livellara had recently confessed in his own town but he went to Padre Pio's confessional more than anything to ask him to pray for his mother's health.

---

[80]   S.E., San Giovanni Rotondo 10.4.1991.
[81]   Cassano Murge (BA) 27.4.1995.

He tells us: "After receiving absolution, as I was getting up to leave the Padre stopped me and said: "For that other thing, break it off, break it off immediately!".

And I, understanding what the Padre was alluding to said: "But Father, I want to. I pray, I try very hard".

And the Saint: "Break it off immediately!".

"Yes" I answered. And I went away.

"That thing" the Padre hinted at, was the relationship I had with a girl. I had met her and had fallen in love with her so deeply I wanted to marry her. But after a year we had been seeing each other, she confessed she was already married. I was very upset. I tried to leave her, but I couldn't.

To Padre Pio I hadn't said anything to not complicate my request for the grace of good health for my mother. I had only spoken about "that thing" in confession at Venice, where I lived. I returned home. The girl was called to Bologna for family reasons. I didn't see her again"[82].

6. At San Giovanni Rotondo the Franciscan Third Order aided the poor and delivered whatever charity donated. One day a nice piece of cloth was delivered to a girl who gave a helping hand, and as she was also not very well off, she took it to make herself a dress.

She went to Confession and Padre Pio immediately at the beginning of the sacramental dialogue said to her: "You have got dirty hands!".

She not understanding what the Padre wanted to say answered: "No father, I have washed them".

And the Saint: "And what about that material you kept for yourself?".

---

[82] Luciano Livellare, Chiavari 4.12.1994.

"But it was from the things for the poor, and I am poor", added the girl.

The Padre wanting to make himself clear said: "Yes, but you should have asked"[83].

7. Maria Mansi narrates what happened to her mother. Since she had to go from Biella to Gioia del Colle, her hometown, she decided to pay a visit to San Giovanni Rotondo to speak to the Padre. She went, confessed and told him that she had missed Mass the Sunday before, "Because it was raining heavily".

"Yes, but when you left on your journey to come here it was raining too", pointed out Padre Pio[84].

8. R. Rossi was in the queue waiting to confess to Padre Pio. Before her was an elderly lady talking to the Saint.

Whilst waiting her turn, she made a hasty examination of her conscience. But although she examined herself carefully, she couldn't find any sins. She kept saying to herself: "Well, to think about it I haven't harmed anyone and I have no idea what I should say to this Holy Man".

Whilst she was locked in her thoughts, the penitent who had gone before her ended her Confession and approached her by saying: "Padre Pio said that, if you don't stop acting so arrogantly, he won't confess you".

As if struck by lightening the woman didn't have the time to go near the confessional. She left and didn't ever go back. But, to those who went near her to ask why she hadn't confessed,

---

[83] *Notes on Padre Pio*, taken from the stories of a few spiritual daughters who wish to remain anonymous, San Giovanni Rotondo, 30.9.1994.
[84] Maria Mansi, Biella, 29.11.1999.

she said that she hadn't acknowledged a child she had before getting married, and that she had taken part in séances[85].

9. Serafina, Quasetto Tosetti confessed to Padre Pio for the first time in 1949. When Padre Pio opened the grate, he said to her. "Go and confess to somebody else". And she went to another priest.

Even the second time she had made the journey to San Giovanni without any success. She had booked to confess to the Padre, hoping she would be able to, and having a weeks' time to wait, however her time ended and she had to return to Biella. Before leaving San Giovanni Rotondo a fellow who had heard her mentioning her disappointment, offered to telegraph her when it was the day turn.

After about ten days the telegram arrived and she went once more to San Giovanni Rotondo. Heaven had rewarded her constancy. Before she entered the confessional she wrote a note about the things she wanted to ask at the end of Confession. But when the moment arrived to tell Padre Pio her problems as a mother to receive advice and comfort, her mind went blank and she couldn't say a word.

The Saint, after giving her absolution with fatherly love, touched on all the points she had written on the paper, enlightening her about what to do[86].

10. That the Padre acted under the guidance of the Holy Spirit, both in comforting and reprimanding, was shown to Anna Baroni by a prodigious sign.

"One day", she says, "I confessed to Padre Pio and I asked

---

[85] Ida Cassano, Cesena 26.5.1999.
[86] Serafina Auaretto Tosetti, Biella 29.11.1999.

his advice about something that was of great importance in my life. He gave me an answer but it was not the one I wanted. I repeated my question adding other details which seemed important to me. Once more the Padre answered negatively. When for the third time I returned to the subject to get him on my side I heard a scream: "But are you mad?". I was upset and said to myself feeling sad and deluded: this time the Padre hasn't understood me and he's been impolite!

After the absolution, perturbed and dismayed I went, as penitents used to do, in front of the confessional to kiss his hand. As soon as he moved the curtain he appeared transfigured: his face was bright and beautiful and an aura of splendour was around him. In an instant my soul became completely calm after that answer from Heaven".

At a distance of years, after Padre Pio had left us, Anna with nostalgia and regret says: "If I could only have the fortune again to kneel at his feet and ask him: "Father, tell me, am I alright in God's eyes? Am I living as he wills?". Yes, the Padre showed us even only with a glance if the Lord was with us"[87].

11. One testimony, that of Quirino Cresti from Chiavari, seems to be a brief summary of the charismatic elements that characterized Padre Pio's way of confessing.

He says: "Padre Pio quickly gave the impression to know you intimately. He had his own method to not lose your attention. The first time I met him in a brief conversation I had been allowed, he treated me well. I complained about unfairness at work and he agreed with me.

Some time later I went to Confession but he sent me away because I hadn't respected my mother. This sin he saw through

---

[87]   Anna Baroni, Chiavari 17.9.1995.

the light of the Holy Spirit, because I hadn't spoken about it.

Another time, always in Confession whilst I wanted to speak freely to him, he stopped me, saying "Do you think before you speak?". And made me understand that sometimes with a careless word you can lose a friendship or a job. He had guessed that I was hot-tempered and not patient.

He insisted on charity.

Every time I spoke of marriage he discouraged me. Once I was going out with a girl from Bergamo and I wanted to talk about this in Confession, but he said to me: "There are many things of more importance!". Another time I started to speak about another girl: "Don't make me waste time" he said in a hasty way.

I never got married[88].

We must not think that the charism of being able to see into one's soul, which the Padre made use of, in the cases we have presented, could be a constant quality. We know that the charism is given to help other and that the Holy Spirit gives it depending on circumstances and needs.

Padre Pio needed to call on the indispensable lights of his preparation and experience to carry out his priestly ministry. By no means, the least thing he was called on his diligence in listening and analysing the situation; and the Saint used it paying attention to what the penitent had to say, waiting for the light that would come from on high.

A well respected affirmed professional person narrates the following: "I had the grace to confess to Padre Pio: I complained about my family situation, particularly my wife who was always aggressive and hard. That Holy Man let me speak for longer than he usually let other speak, maybe ten minutes,

---

[88]   Quirino Cresti, Chiavari 28.9.1995.

without saying a word. I spoke and cried, he listened.

At a certain point, like thunder he shouted: "Change your life! Say ten Gloria in honour of St. Michael". He absolved me but I was shocked and upset about how the Confession had ended.

After saying my penance, I went out of the church and the friend who had come with me asked how it had gone. I let him understand I preferred not to talk because I felt like a wounded animal. We set off on our way back.

As we went my upset started to give way to peace and joy. Near the Friary of the Capuchin Friars Minor of San Marco in Lamis, that is a few kilometres away from San Giovanni Rotondo I stopped the car and said to my friend: "A hundred psychologists and psychiatrists couldn't have given a more enlightened answer, more truthful about such a twisted situation, that needed only silence and acceptation".

I had the certainty that the Padre had interpreted that tangle not seeing it in an intellectual way but with the light that came from God[89].

Therefore, the Holy Spirit remained always at his side. It belongs to the inner reading of the soul, "the insight of the spirit" which is defined as "a charismatic insight in judging the honesty of the words and works of others"[90]. This happens, when the Holy Spirit gives a person a particular enlightenment through which he can arrive at the truth from a particular intuition.

We will return on the subject of Padre Pio's charismatic behaviour in a separate chapter.

---

89 This testimony was listened to in Morcone (BN) on 14.11.1994 from the voice of a witness who prefers to remain anonymous.
90 P. Rossano in *Le Lettere di San Paolo*, Ed. Paoline 1988, 163 note 10.

d) Care and attention in carrying out God's will

One day a girl from Trento had received from Padre Pio, through me, a piece of advice about her future; she had asked if she should continue to go out with a boy who was a non-believer, and make plans to get married. The Padre had answered with a definite no.

Once she got home, seeing how things had turned out and with fresh doubts in her mind, she wanted to question the Saint again and wrote him a letter.

In the office for correspondence the letter came by chance into my hands. I brought the content of the letter to the Padre's attention and he answered cuttingly: "Padre Pio only speaks once"[91].

1. The testimony of Wanda Sellach shows us a Padre just as sure of his actions.

She says: "I had convinced a girl to go and confess to Padre Pio, but he sent her away. I didn't give up. It was during the war and at that time booking to confess to Padre Pio didn't exist, so the next day I took her to church again and pushed her near the confessional, but once again the Padre dismissed her.

When he had finished confessing, I went to the Saint, who was saying goodbye to us before re-entering the Friary and remonstrated about the way he had treated my young friend. He answered: "When I start with no, it's no".

Then almost to calm me, impatient interlocutor, down, he added: "Besides, that girl is like coal. When it's out it stains when it's lit it burns"[92].

---

[91] See the particulars of this case p. 133.
[92] Sara Sellach, San Giovanni Rotondo 7.12.1995.

2. Sr. Maristella Magistrali, of the Franciscan Missionary Nuns of the Word made Flesh, was struck by the coherence of the answers given by Padre Pio to the same questions asked to him in two different moments of time.

She said: "In Spring of 1968, returning from Uganda where I had lived for nine years, I was allowed by my superiors to go with my mother to San Giovanni Rotondo to meet Padre Pio. I confessed to the Padre and after receiving absolution I asked him five questions. He, with patience and goodness listened to me, sometimes asking me to repeat what I had said. And he answered all I asked him.

After Confession, to be sure that the Saint had understood me, I spoke to Fr. Pellegrino and asked him to re-read to Padre Pio the questions that I had brought to his attention. In the afternoon I met the Padre's faithful companion and he gave me the note with the answers I wished: they were exactly the same that the Saint had given me in words"[93].

3. The following episode took place out of the confessional, but we are adding it as it is in the same light as the preceding ones.

One day Fr. Dalmazio Lombardi from Morcone, Vicar of the Friary of San Giovanni Rotondo went to Padre Pio with a letter that had arrived from the United States of America. The parents of an American soldier who had fought in Vietnam and had been declared missing, wanted to know if they could have continued to hope they could once more embrace their son.

Padre Pio listened, stayed silent for a while, then asked:

"How many years have gone by since they had any news?

"Five Father", answered Fr. Dalmazio.

---

[93]   Sr. Maristella Magistrali, Sassuolo 24.9.1999.

Padre Pio stayed for an moment closed within himself and then answered: "I believe there is no more hope". The conversation ended there.

After a few days, the confrère who was embarrassed to give such an answer, neared Padre Pio once more and asked: "Father, but can I take away from two parents the hope of seeing their son again? It's like telling them their son is dead".

And the Saint: "My son, I said what I think. You answer as you think fit"[94].

From the way the Padre behaved in Confession or even in giving advice or suggestions, it was easy to understand that he had an inner certainty: that of speaking in God's name.

The Padre between charism and prayer

We have observed that charism being a gift, it cannot be a permanent talent in one of the Lord's servants, but it is coupled with the carrying out of a mission. Sometimes the Spirit does not immediately offer enlightenment.

If Heaven is silent, the charismatic man must also turn to prayer to beseech light for himself and for others until in every circumstance and for each person God's will is carried out.

One day, Fr. Carmelo Durante, Superior of the Friary asked Padre Pio some advice about how to behave in a particular situation, the Saint answered he would pray.

A few days later the confrère asked his the same thing again and the Padre assured him once more that he had put the matter

---

[94] Fr. Tommaso Plenzio da Morcone, S. Marco La Catola (FG) 30.12.1998.

before God.

Finally Padre Pio gave an answer but the Guardian Father seemed quite surprised at the time he had had to wait. The Saint said: "My son, if the answer doesn't come from above what can I myself say?"[95].

That the Padre couldn't always give instant prophetic replies, that is bring us God's word and tell us about it at will, is confirmed by Fr. Eusebio Notte who one day asked him the reason why this was not possible. The Saint, lifting his hand towards Heaven, answered: "If nobody up there says something, what answers can I give?"[96].

In these cases not even the long experience of director and master of spirit was enough to suggest adequate answers to the various situations.

We must not marvel at this, charisms is the exception, prayer is the norm in the way to arrive at truth. It is in this view we must see the invitation to prayer that the Padre at times gave to those who turned to him for advice.

With regards to this we will give just one example. Sr. Rosetta Paparella says: "From the age of 15-16 I felt the religious call but I was gripped with doubt. "Will I be able to be successful?", I asked myself. I went to Padre Pio and in Confession I told him of my state of mind. "Pray, pray to the Holy Spirit, that all will mature, my dear daughter", was his answer.

I passed in front of the confessional to kiss his hand and waited a moment because I wanted a clearer answer. He fatherly said "Go, dear daughter" putting his hand on my head.

After a few months I returned to tell him I was certain I had

95 Fr Carmelo Durante, Larino Summer 1986.
96 Fr. Eusebio Notte, Isernia 22.12.1999.

a vocation for the religious life and was confident that I would be fine. After telling my sins I opened my soul. "Father I wish to leave, but we are a large family with nine children and my elder sister has to get married; my parents say, according to the custom in our village, she has to leave our house before I do".

Padre Pio replied: "When God calls you, there is no time to wait. Go in peace with my blessing".

I then asked if all would go well with my sister's wedding and he said: "You think about yourself and don't worry about your sister".

In the space of a few months I got everything ready and left to fulfil my dream.

My sister got married after seven years: "If I had had to wait for her to leave the house before I did, perhaps I would have betrayed God's call"[97].

Listening to God

Another means that the Saint used, to arrive at the truth, was the attention he paid to God's word to discover his Divine Will. His diligence in this was quite extraordinary.

Fr. Atanasio Lonardo from Teano, Capuchin, who one day had preached in Padre Pio's presence at the little church of San Giovanni Rotondo, writes: "I wish to underline an aspect of his life, which perhaps has not been touched by the numerous biographies. He was as hungry for the divine Eucharist as he was for God's word, which he tried to listen to: weather it was given by great or poor orators or if it was preached by the humblest priest was of little interest to him.

---

[97] Sr. Rosetta Paparella , Corigliano D'Otranto 5.11.1986.

Always devoured and absorbed, many times kneeling, he seemed to hang on the preacher's lips, who for him as St. Augustin says, likewise St. Francis was a channel of Grace. If the channel was of gold, silver or humble clay, as in my case, was of no importance. The same Grace that washes ,purifies, sanctifies and fecundates always flowed"[98].

That Padre Pio did not disdain even the most simple announcer of God's word is confirmed by another testimony.

1. Fr. Marcello Lepore, a young priest from the brotherhood of San Giovanni Rotondo, was given the job, by the Frather Guardian, of preaching a triduum for the feast of St. Antony of Padua. Padre Pio who was always present when the community met together, listened to him and then said: "Good, you have a good memory"[99].

2. Fr. Cipriano Di Meo, from Serracapriola was a novice priest and in 1949 came to San Giovanni Rotondo to serve in the fraternity. One day, in the refectory Fr Agostino from San Marco in Lamis asked if there was anyone among the priests who was prepared to preach for the feast of St. Francis. As no one offered after a moment of silence the young priest's name was proposed. He accepted even if he felt rather embarrassed to speak in church in front of Padre Pio. After the sermon the Padre went to meet him to give him the *posit*, and whist Fr. Cipriano played down the compliment saying he was a beginner, the padre embraced him and said: "As a beginner, you have reached the *optimu*"[100].

3. A similar thing happened to me and Padre Pio was not

---

[98] Testimony written by Fr. Atanasio Lonardo, Capuchin who lived with Padre Pio at San Giovanni Rotondo.
[99] Fr. Marcello Lepore, Foggia 11.3.1997.
[100] Fr. Cipriano Di Meo, San Severo (FG), 6.4.1922.

lacking in fatherly appreciation.

In the September of 1954 after a few months of holy priest-hood, I was at San Giovanni Rotondo and the Guardian Father asked me to speak in church during Vespers. I remember I chose the theme of prayer, showing the aspect of the souls elevation towards God. It was neither more nor less that a scholarly exercise. I remember that I pointed out that speaking of the soul, in this case I meant the heart.

The Padre in the sacristy found the way to congratulate me: "Good, you spoke well when you said the heart must be lifted up to God when one prayers".

However we must note that as well as being attentive he was also critical. To a young brother at the end of one of his reflections given in church he said: "Lad, you have got to prepare yourself a bit better than that.

"But Padre Pio's attention was not only limited to hearing God's word in his research for truth. Fr. Pellegrino writes: "Often, during conversations, he was thin king about the solution to one of his own inner problems, but he continued listening, almost to find some help in his brother's opinions. Sometimes he asked one to repeat a phrase which he thought particularly interesting for his own reflections[101].

With regards to this the same confrère offers us another testimony. One day Padre Pio speaking to him about the virtue and wisdom of Bro. Costantino of the brotherhood of San Giovanni Rotondo and mentioning other good souls said: "To me these Brothers-in-faith always say something on behalf of the Holy Virgin, on behalf of the Church and on behalf of God".

---

[101] Fr. Pellegrino Funicelli, *La prudenza esige il rischio*, in "Voce di Padre Pio" monthly magazine of the postulation of the beatification cause of Padre Pio of Pietrelcina, Capuchin Friary "Our Lady of Grace", 71043 San Giovanni Rotondo, FG, July 1979, 12.

Fr. Pellegrino concluded: "The last expression struck me in particular: therefore he listened to certain people's words as if he were listening to God"[102].

To explain this way of listening which was always present in Padre Pio, we must take note that he continually underwent a distressing test: the Saint lived with the "atrocious" doubt as to whether what he did "in the course of his life" was "pleasing to God's liking; that is whether there was in his actions an offence against God"[103].

4. The therapy of waiting

Padre Pio, we have seen, many times sent penitents away from the confessional with the irrefutable "Go away!". But in sending a brother away, he wished to use a particular therapy called *"the penance of waiting"* and which he considered very important. The first reason, the most obvious of why he used this method, was because the penitent was not completely ready for the meeting with God.

To follow the way to sanctity it is necessary to change one's way of life, a "spiritual metamorphosis" as the Padre said, which shows the conversation has taken place. But spiritual masters underline that people cannot change their habits, if they do not change their mentality, which they call *metanoia*[104].

And Padre Pio is sure that waiting makes one meditate by putting ideas in order, and it teaches the humility of the heart.

---

[102] P. Pellegrino Funicelli, *Le guide delle anime*, in *Voce di Padre Pio*, May 1981, 10-11.

[103] Cf. *Letters I*, 1053, 26 September 1917.

[104] We will treat this subject later on, see p. 97 onwards.

He used to say: "It is in this way one learns to beg for God's mercy"[105].

One day Fr. Pellegrino asked Padre Pio in a different way about his usual objection to the ease with which he refused absolution and said: "Father, you, helped by many praying souls, work hard to bring back souls who have fallen away to the heart of the Church. At the same time you leave them for months without absolution. Doesn't this mean you leave them out of the Church?".

The Padre answered: "It isn't enough to enter the Church. You need to come in well. For you it is enough that they enter in Mass. For me it's important they are well prepared to come in. The months used to prepare one to be part of the Church are well spent. Entering unprepared is just the same as not entering"[106].

But we must point out that this theory was sometimes used by the Saint even with those, who for the sincerity of their repentance or the seriousness of their proposals, he thought were ready to meet God, or with others that he was convinced already lived in Divine Grace.

Fr. Pellegrino one day said: "Father, those people that you do not absolve, in the case of sudden death, run the risk of damnation".

Padre Pio answered: "But who told you that these souls are in God's bad books!?".

The questioner objected: "And if they are not in God's bad books why can't they approach the Eucharist?".

---

[105] *Marian Month*, day 5.
[106] P. Pellegrino Funicelli, *Croce Nera e vesti bianche*, in *Voce di Padre Pio*, October 1981, 12.

The Padre replied: "Because they have to do a particular penance"[107].

The young confrère then observed that this penance was a "little" refined and for this, perhaps reserved for the souls who were able to understand its efficiency and importance".

We are not able to fully understand or give explanations about the Holy Confessor's way of confessing. A spiritual daughter says that the Padre made the souls he wished to raise higher, go through a passive purification, which could not be part of their plans or possibilities but only in the projects of the Spirit, rather similar to that reserved to some saints that God wished to lead to a more intimate union with him.

Fr. Pellegrino reveals that in the apostolic work carried out by the Padre there was something mysterious that could not be seen or controlled completely rationally. He writes: "Once I said: "Father, you make a black cross on the white clothes of the penitent, in short like a seal.

"That's right", he answered, without letting me know if he was joking or not"[108].

This "particular penance", demanded by the Padre for some penitents, which was terrible, also included not being able to take communion. Once Fr. Pellegrino wanted to talk about this to the Saint.

He told him that as a high school student he usually confessed to Fr. Benedetto Nardella, who had been Padre Pio's spiritual director.

One day this enlightened spiritual director after listening to his holy confession gave him absolution, but soon after made

---

[107] *Ibid.*, 13.
[108] *Ibid.*

the following imposition: "Tomorrow you must not take communion because in the last three Confessions you admitted the same sin".

At the end of this story Padre Pio commented: "Obviously you didn't appreciate you spiritual blessing enough". With this deprivation Fr. Benedetto wanted to encourage you to appreciate them a little more. The punishment is "hellish" but necessary to make the Church's children less unworthy and more presentable"[109].

Saying this the Padre gave a glimmer to understand the aim of this method. There is also to say that once he felt the terrible suffering of being deprived of communion. He who lived for the Eucharist! Fr. Pellegrino tells us that one day during recreation, talking to the Saint about the education methods used at the beginning of the previous century, in the novitiate of the Capuchins of Morcone, he said: "One day the Master Friar of the novices said without any reason: "Tomorrow there will be no communion for you".

The confrères who were listening to Padre Pio's story didn't have time to make a s comment because he, burst into tears, and Fr. Pellegrino and another confrère had to accompany him back to his cell to live again "in bitter solitude a punishment he had suffered 50 years before"[110].

The Padre, therefore, well aware that he, putting off absolution for a period whether short or long, made the penitent go through a red hot purifying melting pot. Fr. Pellegrino too experienced this and clearly showed he felt the weight

---

[109] P. Pellegrino Funicelli, *Arciconfraternita della buona morte*, in *Voce di Padre Pio*, December 1981, 13.
[110] *Ibid.*, p. 12-13.

of this punishment by protesting. But Padre Pio said to him one day: "My son, I understand that to be your benefactor, I must be a kind of tyrant: When I make the first sign of the cross on a penitent, I seem to be the crucifier and he the crucified".

Then, almost to excuse himself of the suffering caused to those who went to him to be reconciled with God, he added: "It's true I make my penitents sweat blood. However, I also add my own blood"[111].

That it cost blood to return souls to grace through his apostolic actions, carried out in the confessional was well known by those who lived with him in the Friary. An episode I found noted in my diary confirms this.

"On 3 September 1965 Padre Pio returning to his room soon after Mass, asked for a bit of breathing space, before going to the Ladies' confessional. Whilst he was being helped to lie down on his bed by myself and Fr. Onorato Marcucci, he said: "Let's have five minutes rest before I go down into the church. Today I don't really feel up to confessing".

We told him that, as he was so tired, for his benefit and for the benefit of the people it would be better if he saved himself that morning for later. But he wouldn't take our advice. As we insisted that he stayed in his room, at the end he said: "Well, then I shouldn't go down every morning. It's useless to try and rest after I've bled myself dry!".

We then closed the shutters of the two little windows and went out.

But not even a minute had passed when we heard him call: "Come on and get this lazy-bones off the bed". We went in and

---

[111] *Marian Month*, day 9.

decided to take him down to church for the Confession.

In the corridor we met Fr. Clemente di Postiglione who asked the Padre how he was and he answered: "I can bear no more"[112].

Essential preparation elements

In first position as a means to reconciliation with the Holy Father, Padre Pio puts prayer as a cry for mercy and an impetration for divine forgiveness.

Prayer

We read in the Marian Month that the diligent Confessor "intended to make penitents waiting for an absolution pray a lot". Fr. Pellegrino notes: "Effectively the major part of those who did not receive it, began to quickly feel an inner torment that was so strong they felt impelled to call on all the saints to intercede for them and not only but also the help of their brothers joined in prayer. It happened therefore as a mutual assistance of prayer[113].

We must reveal however that even here the Padre preceded the penitents. He was in first place in this beseeching crusade, ready to obtain mercy and forgiveness from Heaven. "You can't imagine", he said to Fr. Pellegrino, how much and how often I pray for those penitents to whom I have imposed a just

---

[112] Personal Diary.
[113] *Marian Month*, day 6.

and beneficial penance, even if it appears to be too harsh"[114].

In his task to save sinners the Saint involved some of his spiritual children, of whom he expressively asked help.

He did so also with the same Fr. Pellegrino, when at the end of his confession he once gave as a penance, and not for the first time, a collection of prayers with a long list of names and addresses which was impossible to remember.

The Padre also included in the list the names of those he intended his confrère to pray for. Since Fr. Pellegrino objected to this, Padre Pio added: "You ask that they pray following my intentions. Who knows they can be caught in a snare and therefore, pray for their own conversion"[115].

Fr. Pellegrino lets us know that one of the people who Padre Pio turned to, to beg for prayers was Bro. Costantino (a friar who was not a priest, who for many years had gone from door to door looking for the bread of charity for the friars).

Padre Pio said: "Bro. Costantino, as old and as ill as he is, seems as if he is no longer worth anything. And yet as an obedient son of the Holy Mother Church, he is worth more than you and me.

Do you know why he has so much peace within his soul?

Because he has put all his trust in the Holy Virgin and because he is at least interested as possible about earthly problems, which you consider to be very important. His spirit of oration and his devotion to the Holy Virgin are virtues which wash away all human defects and weaknesses and if it were possible would put out the flames of Hell".

And finally he added: "This man attracts Our Lady's gaze and his prayers are the salvation of many souls.

---

[114] *Ibid.*
[115] *Marian Month*, day 13.

You believe that penitents are attracted by Confession and I say it is not so, they are pushed to repentance by these hidden prayers. I don't speak like this for stupid humility. It's the truth. How is it possible that men change heart and mind. For the fame of the confessor? You really don't understand a thing if you believe this!

Certain hearts can only be softened in the presence of our Heavenly Mother; she listens to these sons and daughters devoted of the Holy Church and comes down to earth. I would almost say that she becomes strong from the prayers of these men that you consider useless"[116].

Meditation and Reflection

The prayer Padre Pio expected from the penitents, whilst they were waiting to be reconciled with God, he wished to be part of a moment of reflection and meditation.

Today, speaking of spiritual retreats, we use the expression *"to have the desert's experience"*, meaning the isolating of oneself for a certain time, to think about one's spiritual reality, immersed in silence far away from the cries of the world. Few Christians however when planning their free time, allow themselves a time which is so important and good for their well-being. Today's men so dedicated to action, are not only incapable of slowing down their frenetic life-style to reflect for a while, but if they are forced to do so for some need or problem, they don't have a moments' peace.

Our Holy Confessor, by putting off absolution also had this

---

[116] P. Pellegrino Funicelli, *La guida delle anime* in *Voce di Padre Pio*, May 1981, 10-11.

aim: to keep some spiritual children far away from their ordinary chores.

He often repeated the idea that, in the path that leads to God,
you cannot set aside the light of faith, and faith needs to mature
through meditation made in silence and solitude. "Without this
light" he said "you must stop: you can't go ahead in the dark.

This is why certain pauses are necessary. You cannot play.
Blind Man's Buff on the path of Christian perfection"[117].

That these are moments in which one does not certainly
indulge in idleness, but instead finds oneself and meets God,
is declared in the Holy Scriptures that caution "stand ye in
the ways, and see and ask for the old paths, where is the good
way and walk therein and ye shall find rest for your souls" (Jer
6.16).

The spiritual masters remind us of this.

St. Anselmo writes: "Come on, wretched mortal, escape for
a short time from your chores, leave your tumultuous thoughts.
Put your busy activities and grave worries to one side for a
moment. Wait a while for God and rest in him. Go deep inside your soul and exclude everything except God and that
which helps you search for him, then close the door and look
for God".

St. John of the Cross explains why this introspective action is needed. "It is to be noted that Jesus, the Word of God
together with the Father and the Holy Spirit essentially and
presently are hidden in the inner part of the soul. Therefore the
soul which wishes to find them, must retreat into itself as if all
the rest didn't exist[118].

---

[117] *Marian Month*, day 7.
[118] St. John of the Cross in *Cantico*, 1, 6; in *Opere*, Roma Postulazione
Generale dei Carmelitani Scalzi, 1959.

Fr. Pellegrino, with regards to the criteria wisely adopted by Padre Pio of making the penitents wait before giving them absolution, had reservations: he thought it valid for some, those who needed to be converted, but he didn't think it was so right when it was applied to those who had already been moving in God's ways and working to help others. He made no secret of this with the Padre and he openly admitted his doubts: "Wouldn't those who have already been walking in God's ways for a while, please Our Lady more by going about, doing good works instead of staying at San Giovanni Rotondo and resting even if it is a spiritual rest?".

The Saint assured him that they "would waste time and they wouldn't have gone forward one inch in their battle. They would be like those statues of bronze or marble that one sees in squares. Then to sum up his thought about the particular moment the soul must live to find God, he added: "You make confusion between chatting-prayer and brain-prayer, it's like confusing mechanical action and action made with soul, dead action and action made lively by grace". And sticking to this point he asserted: "However waiting and pauses are necessary for all".

One of those present at this discussion was the engineer Cremonini from Modena, who came out with the witty remark: "In short you want to really lock us in this golden cage" alluding to the shrine "Our Lady of Grace" of San Giovanni Rotondo".

"Ah no", promptly replied Padre Pio "I want to make you come out of those crazy cages made by your affairs to let you go into a house, the house of our Heavenly Mother"[119].

One of our brothers said in a conference: "President of the industry and manager of Maserati, he had come to San Gio-

---

[119] *Marian Month*, day 7.

vanni Rotondo about fifteen times and had never received absolution". In fact Padre Pio acted in a particular way with him,
which humanely speaking could have seemed "spiteful". For
example, when in a conversation, Mr Cremonini came forward
and made some quip, Padre Pio turned his back and spoke to
someone else.

The engineer angrily returned to Modena; then from Modena
left for the Gargano because "he had to come and say a couple
of vigorous words to Padre Pio". He came here got a "thrash-
ing" and returned to Modena and it went on for months.

Finally he was absolved[120], he became one of the Padre's
family, faithful to the promise he had made to live a truly
Christian life[121].

5. The returns

Pope John Paul II during the sermon held on the day of Padre Pio's canonization, after revealing that "the Ministry of the
Confession, which constituted one of the distinctive traits of
his apostolate, attracted innumerable crowds of faithful to the
friary of San Giovanni Rotondo, underlined: "Even when that
Singular Confessor treated the pilgrims with apparent harshness, they, realising the gravity of their sins and sincerely repentant, nearly always went back for the pacifying embrace of
sacramental forgiveness[122].

Some of the episodes which have been previously narrated
are proof of what the Pope affirmed. But we must say that the

---

[120] This will be seen in detail later on.
[121] Lecture given to the confrères in san Giovanni Rotondo on 18th April
1985.
[122] The Osservatore Romano, 17-18 June 2002.

pilgrims treated "with apparent harshness", not only returned to him but becoming his spiritual children chose the Padre as their normal guide, and consulted him regularly for their spiritual needs.

Here are some cases which we wish to add for a further documentation, even if is always only partial.

1. Teodoro Grossrubatcher, a lumberjack from the Dolomites in January 1967 left Selva di Val Gardena to go to San Giovanni Rotondo.

Whilst in confession he admitted amongst other things he had lost control of his tongue at the tavern and with his animals.

"How many times?" asked the Padre.

He started to mumble phrases such as: "I don't know" or "I don't remember".

The Padre stopped the Confession saying: "Get out you scoundrel!".

But sending him away from the confessional, Padre Pio had infused a yearning nostalgia for his eyes and words".

So after about ten months on 16 November of the same year, he was once more in the sacristy to say hello to Padre Pio.

"As soon as Padre Pio saw me", he tells us, "before I opened my mouth", he said: "When did you leave your town?".

"Yesterday at ten, father". I answered.. He stared at me for a few seconds and then went on.

A few days later I admitted amongst other things that I had done "*la storna*", that is had too many drinks. He with a tone of voice which was both firm and fatherly said: "Don't do it again!".

I answered "No Father".

"Don't do it again!", repeated the Padre.

Whilst I was renewing my promise and making my mind

up to keep it, I had the clear cut sensation that the Padre was putting an extra-ordinary force within me, to keep me from that damn vice. I never drank again".

Teodoro returned again to Padre Pio in February 1968 to confess, and on 29 June of the same year.

"I didn't manage to confess this last time", he tells us, "but during the Mass I saw the Padre transfigured, his bright eyes and his rosy face shone".

Padre Pio had entered into his life and he would always feel his protection[123].

2. A young man from a town in the North of Italy who was going through a bad period of religious crisis heard Fr. Mariano Paladino, who came from the Friary of Padre Pio, speaking, and was inspired to confide in him. The priest, after listening to him made him a proposal: why not come down to San Giovanni Rotondo to talk to the Padre".

He accepted and arriving in the Gargano, decided to go to Confession.

Before he opened his mouth Padre Pio said to him: "Answer yes or no to the question I ask".

And the Padre began an examination of conscience: "Have you done this?", asked the Holy Confessor naming a sin. If the youth wanted to say something that was not either approval or disapproval, the Padre repeated: "You have to tell me only yes or no" and continued the examination.

And the Padre gave a list of sins to which the youth unfortunately had to answer only yes. At the end of the exam, the Padre said: "My son, with all these bad sins I can't give you

---

[123] Teodoro Grossrubatcher from Ortisei, Selva di Val Gardena (BZ) 25.11.1993.

absolution" and he sent him away.

The penitent went away crying.

He cried for three days, but during this time the Padre did not abandon him.

One day the Saint passed by him, the young man smelt a wave of perfume. He couldn't understand why, but noticing that Padre Pio had just shaved his tonsure, he thought: "this friar has been to the Barbers' and they have covered him in aftershave.

Going into his hotel whilst he was locked in his thoughts looking at a wall, he saw a photo of the Padre: he was so struck by his penetrating glance that he had to close his eyes. When he re-opened them the photo had disappeared.

He was very surprised and wanted to know what was happening to him. He asked the hotel keeper: "Wasn't there a picture here?". And the keeper answered: "There has never been a picture with photo there".

The young man understood that the Padre was near him in that difficult moment of his life.

He went home feeling calmer. After a period of reflection he went down again to san Giovanni Rotondo. He confessed to the Padre and helped by him made a radical choice: to embrace the religious life and become a priest[124].

3. Probo Vaccarini also had to wait a while before becoming a spiritual son. But it was the Padre who called him.

The first time he approached the confessional he was sent away. Whilst he was telling his sins the Padre had asked him: "How many times?".

---

[124] The witness prefers to remain anonymous. Testimony of December 1999.

He answered "I don't know, when it happens".

And Padre Pio: "Get out. Do you want to go to Hell?".

Even though he was terrorized. He had the strength to ask: "When can I come back?".

"When you are ready", replied the Padre.

Despite this opening by the Saint to continue a dialogue Probo was upset and returning home said to himself: "I'm not going to go back to that friar anymore".

But one night he dreamt of Padre Pio who said to him: "Come and confess yourself", adding a certain examination of conscience.

He went down again to San Giovanni Rotondo, now he knew what he had to confess. When however he was near to the confessional he thought that the number indicated by the Padre in his dream was a little too high and decided to reduce it.

But as soon as he started to confess his faults at the first admittance the Padre shouted at him to be more precise. He understood that he still didn't have the conscience of sin and after being absolved, he methodically followed the Padre's teaching[125].

4. In a most unusual way the Saint cancelled the idea of never returning again to San Giovanni Rotondo from Lorenzo Barale's mind.

Lorenzo from Turin tells us: "My mother had been encouraging me to Padre Pio for a while, but I had no intention of taking up her suggestion.

In the July of 1948 me and some of my friends decided to go to Rimini for a holiday. One evening I felt a strong desire within me to listen to the advice my mother had given me and I said to all those who were with me that the next day I was go-

---

[125] Probo Vaccarini, Rimini 14.5.1998.

ing to leave for San Giovanni Rotondo. I invited them to come with me, but no one accepted my proposal.

When I arrived on the Gargano, after a few days I went to confession.

"Father, I have sworn", I said admitting my first sin.

As soon as he heard this, he shouted: "Go away!".

I got up and went back to the sacristy, almost hiding myself amongst those who were around the confessional.

When Padre Pio finished confessing, he set off to go back to the friary through an opening made amongst the people who greeted him and kisses his hand. I, who was a few metres away, watching him go past said to myself: "Now, we'll see if you see me again! Whist my friends are having a good time in Rimini I came here, and you kicked me out. You won't see me again!".

I hadn't finished thinking this when I suddenly saw the Padre in front of me. He strongly tapped me on the head with his fingertips, bum, bum, bum. Then he went away.

The following year I went to San Giovanni Rotondo again to speak to him. I confessed and after receiving absolution I said: "Father, I'd like to get married and have a large family". I said this without thinking as I had no plans about marriage: I flitted about with girls and I had only just met my wife and she knew nothing about my slight interest in her.

The Padre looked at me and said: "Soon, soon!". After a few years my floating about was over and I was happily married[126].

---

[126] Lorenzo Barale, Genova 19.4.1995.

An immediately perceived message

It must be noticed that the penitent who was harshly rebuked by the Holy Confessor, sometimes instantly understood the ugliness of the state of his soul and the gravity of the offences towards God through a life without morals. His heart was filled with compunction.

1. A man who though himself a good Christian, once during work swore against God. He felt terrible afterwards because it had never happened before.

Some years later he went to confess to Padre Pio and didn't mention this sin which he had completely forgotten. After listening to his sins the Padre asked him if he had anything else to add. When he answered no he said: "Go and ask God's forgiveness for offending him by taking his sacred name in vain".

The poor man went away from the confessional crying for the pain of that sin which was never to appear again in his lifetime[127].

2. Umberto Iorio from Morcone (BN) had heard his family speaking about Padre Pio and he fad felt the desire to meet him. He went up to San Giovanni Rotondo and approached the confessional in which the Padre received the penitents.

"Do you sometimes go to Mass on Sundays?", asked the confessor.

"Sometimes", answered the penitent. And the Padre, "Why, do you live in the desert?", then added: "Go to Mass and then come back".

Umberto who could have been twenty-four or twenty-five years old, got up casually from the kneeling stool, without

---

[127] Testimony given in Campobasso on 23.9.2001.

making a sign, almost indifferently, he went down the corridor to the exit. But as soon as he found himself in the little square in front of the Friary, he suddenly started sobbing.

He states: "I felt inside that I had done something very wrong. Then once I returned home I started to go to Mass every Sunday. I can assure you that up until now I have never missed Mass on Sunday or Holy days of Obligation. Naturally after a few months I returned to Padre Pio to whom by then I felt attached"[128].

3. The following testimony is from a spiritual daughter who defines her first Confession with Padre Pio as an unhappy meeting.

Being a timid young girl, when the Padre opened the grate of the confessional, she found it difficult to speak; then, to the Saint's repeated question, she confided that she often had impure thoughts and images in her mind. The Confessor interrupted her exclaiming: "You had all this filth in your mind and you weren't saying anything?". And he sent her away.

She left feeling very low and, introverted, she went back to the house where she was staying. During the night she was filled with a wave of perfume. She had heard from friends that unusual phenomena meant the Padre was close at hand.

She felt heartened thinking that Padre Pio hadn't refused her, but he was keeping her joined to him inviting her to return.

She didn't lose heart and returned after a few days to the Saint to confess. When amongst the other things she touched the problem of the impure thoughts, that she had mentioned the first time she heard him ask: "Did you send them away immediately?". When the penitent answered she had, the Holy

---

[128] Umberto Iorio, Morcone 19.12.2002.

confessor said: "Well, you can rest at peace". And he gave his absolution.

The young woman wondered why she had been treated differently in the second Confession and concluded: "I think the Padre with that scolding wanted to warn me, as I was living a rather dull life, about a danger which if repeated could have been dangerous".

Some time later, when this spiritual daughter had taken the path of total dedication to live a really Christian life, she spoke to the Padre of the usual problem which sprung up despite her constant effort to be faithful to God, feeling sorry for this sin. But the Saint calmed her down.

Once the Padre said: "They, the impure thoughts, irritate, but they don't harm. Imagine going far down a road and a little dog follows you barking and he wants to hurt you. You turn round and send him away but he comes back. What harm has he done? He has only irritated you and this irritation you must offer to the Lord"[129].

Going back after...forty years

A spiritual son of Padre Pio tells us: "In 1950, when I was 19, I went to San Giovanni Rotondo as I was curious to meet the friar with stigmata.

In the morning I got up early to go to Mass and one day I booked to go to Confession. But when it was my turn I approached the confessional without any preparation, with superficiality and almost indifference. As soon as I knelt down, before I had opened my mouth the Padre in a severe tone

---

[129] S. Martino in Pensilis (CB) 13.12.2002.

shouted: "Go away!". I left without any worry.

From that date I didn't confess again, and later, having become a representative for "Lane Rossi (Rossi Wool)" I passed by Foggia several times without ever feeling the desire to go up to San Giovanni Rotondo again.

Around 1990 at a distance of forty years, the thought of Padre Pio began to spring up again in my mind, it grew until it became a torment. In the morning I woke up early and heard the Saint's voice within me that repeated: "Go away!".

I started to feel the wish to confess but I did nothing to change or ask for forgiveness.

In 1994 I decided to go to a priest. What could I say after such a long time? I made a rough guess at my sins, but after being absolved I didn't feel peaceful.

One day I heard a conference about Padre Pio's spirituality held by the Capuchins who lived with the Saint. I asked to speak to him and with his help I re-examined all my life. I finally found peace.

The Padre had not abandoned me to my destiny of perdition[130].

These cases tell us that Padre Pio did not send penitents away from confession to throw them in the waste basket.

6. The Padre's aim is conversion

It was December 31st 1960 and many spiritual children had gone up to San Giovanni Rotondo to wish the Padre a happy New Year.

---

[130] Ivone Mendo, *Thiene* 21.5.1996.

In the evening, as he usually did, the Saint went to the window of his cell to wave to the little crowd that punctually gathered in the field in front of his window, to say goodnight. The air was biting cold. The Padre to the thanks and greetings added heartfelt words saying: Go home, go home my children, don't catch cold. Good night".

Whilst he was making the sign of the cross once more over all the present he heard a door open and a brother let in a spiritual child who was very close to the Padre and whose affection was returned. The Padre turned round and we, who were around him, noticed that he was quite disturbed to see the visitor.

Re-opening his dialogue with the crowd and totally changing his tone he became serious and said: "If you come to San Giovanni Rotondo to go down again as you arrived it would be better not to come at all".

This message was clearly more directed to the visitor who, hastily saying goodbye to the Padre, left.

We showed our surprise at this unusual coldness by the Padre and he replied: "He has to thank God I didn't treat him worse".

We then realised the spiritual son must have had something that needed to be pardoned that time.

Changing life-style

Constantly immersed in God, the Padre only opened his heart to his confrères to communicate to them the divine richness it contained. He had no aim other that that of being completely at the disposal of all, synthesized by him in the moving words which always affect one when they are repeated "Everyone can say Padre Pio is mine".

Therefore, from those who made him their reference point, he expected a change in their moral behaviour, as if it was not entirely perfectly limpid. "Change your lifestyle", we have seen he shouted to a penitent who blamed others for his un-successes and sadness.

And the change of lifestyle comes through that interior process that the spiritual masters call conversion and that the Catechismo degli Adulti (Catechism for adults) illustrates in a very clear way: "To be converted means to assume a different way of thinking and behaving, putting God and his will first, being ready if necessary to give up any other thing, no matter how important or dear it may be to us. It means to get rid of the idols we have created which bind our heart: welfare, social prestige, cultural and religious prejudice"[131].

The simplest and fullest example to understand the idea of conversion, has been given to us by Jesus in the parable of the prodigal son (cf. Lk. 15, 11-32). In its teaching it underlines: first, that the pleasure-seeking life the young son led, throwing all principles of morality and honesty over his shoulder leads in the end to sadness, misery and loneliness. Second, that the return home to his father's house which gave the unhappy son back his human dignity, illustrated by the "best robe" which must cover his skeleton-like body and "a ring on his hand and shoes on his feet", those feet marked by his wild vain wander-ings, which were completely destructive.

Then there is the feast his father desired, which stands to

---

[131] CONFERENZA EPISCOPALE ITALIANA, *La verità vi farà liberi, Catechismo degli adulti*, Ed. Libreia Editrice Vaticana, Città del Vaticano, 1995, n. 141.

illustrate as well as the fatherly love that "who converts opens to communion and finds again harmony with God, the others and himself: he rediscovers a former blessing that had been waiting for him for a while"[132].

He finds again the joy of living.

A time of celebration at San Giovanni Rotondo

Even in the little church of Our Lady of Grace "there were celebrations" for a son that was reconciled with the Heavenly Father.

Fr. Pellegrino writes: "All those who, after waiting a long time, received absolution from Padre Pio and with this absolution the definite start of a new life, exploded with uncontrollable joy and even if they didn't do it they would have been capable of shouting and singing in church, in the square and in the hotels".

One day, when I had been able to see a moving explosion of this joy for the conversion of a particular soul absolved by Padre Pio, having the opportunity and the right moment I questioned him saying: "Father, it seems as if you remain impassive in these cases, as if you are not disconcerted by either the spiritual storms or the explosions of joy of your penitents. But I am convinced by what I have heard you say and by the difference I note in you in these occasions, to find myself in front of a confessor who does not end his actions with the formula of absolution".

"Yes, that's true, I follow all my penitents as if I have become their shadow. I too feel much joy in my heart and intimately thank God. Just because I do not show this joy I don't

---

[132] *Ibid.*, n. 143.

believe my joy is less than that of my penitents".

"But where do you find these reasons of joy for an absolution you have given?".

"After I have seen in a penitent's behaviour the signs of real repentance, not only can I no longer refuse absolution, but I can give it with great pleasure.

More than this, for me in these cases it is like allowing one a passport for Heaven or permission to visit it, should I say mark out, whilst still on earth a place in Heaven.

It is right at this moment I feel the duty to be the guide of the soul that has been entrusted to me by the Holy Virgin. To accomplish this duty I'd find the way to escape from a prison without doors or windows, and I'd even be able to run away from Heaven, until I was able to deliver back to Our Lady with whom I have a pact, these souls she delivered in my care".

My curiosity was not ended; in fact, it had increased thinking that these reactions were not the norm with other confessors. I was especially thinking of myself and I said so.

He answered: "When there is a real truthful conversion, there is always a reaction of joy shown more or less, who ever is the confessor or the penitent. Real confessors and real penitents are not isolated. In fact they make one heart and one soul".

Then I said: "Here at San Giovanni Rotondo even the sacramental seal comes a cropper".

He laughed at the joke but said: "You can never say you have seen me lose control in this way. You are the ones who go over the top with your celebrations of joy, but you are free to do so and in truth this doesn't displease me".

But the Padre with the confrère who wished to investigate about the impulses of his heart, stressed that the joy of which they were speaking is bound to real conversions: the confessions which do not give guarantees of a change of lifestyle, are for him a source of sadness. He said: "Rather let us reflect on the other thing for which neither you nor the others should feel joyful but instead you should all suffer.

Instead I am the only one to suffer and weep bitterly.

[I speak of] conversions that conserve the characteristics of time and space, that is those conversions which apparently seem sincere, [but] last only a few days or months and are confined to the space of our little church. They are conversions that do not have the seal of a radical and eternal metamorphosis.

For me only these authentic changes, passing from a state of disgrace to a state of Grace in God, give me authentic joy".

The Saint stressed that his joy was not only connected to absolution, but also in the moment he saw the penitent had decided in his heart to change his way of behaving to be in the right condition to be absolved[133].

A radical metamorphosis

Padre Pio therefore wishes each path of faith to be made of a continuous conversion, based on "radical, definite, lasting choices". All his thoughtful work leaned towards this and when he saw that all his care was not followed by the results he hoped for he was much saddened. He put in the "Holiness Fair" as he said the enthusiasm of those who hastened to him.

Once whilst the people in church crowded around him as if he were a saviour, expressing admiration and devotion, making thousands of supplications concerning material goods, the Padre lamented to Fr. Gabriele Bove, who was with him: "there's

---

[133] *Marian Month*, day 21.

not one who has asked to be helped to become a saint".

Fr. Pellegrino seems to have learnt the lesson about conversion desired by Padre Pio well. In a conference entitled "The Priesthood of Padre Pio" to illustrate the kind of change the Saint asked for, he made use of the word "revolution" wishing to say the penitent had to overthrow, upturn, completely change behaviour, habits and actions that up to that moment had characterized and marked his existence.

Our confrère, underlining the Padre's intention to propose this spiritual "revolution" with strength says among the other things: "Once Padre Pio refused a penitent absolution and then said. "If you go and confess to another, you and the one who absolves you will both go to Hell"; as if to say: without a decision to change lifestyle you profane the Sacrament and whoever does so is guilty in the eyes of God. Padre Pio would not accept lukewarm Confessions. I repeat, for him every confession had to be a sign of conversion"[134].

Fr. Pellegrino then, to conclude, gives an example of esteem and fondness with regards to the Saint, which did not have practical reflection from a spiritual point of view.

He says: "Even the poet Gabriele D'Annunzio felt Padre Pio's fascination so much that he wrote him a letter in 1924. D'Annunzio had heard about Padre Pio from a childhood friend, Alfredo Luciani. However, from the simple fact that he never sent the letter, it seems that the writer had no intention of changing his lifestyle"[135].

---

[134] Conference of 18th April 1985; see note 5.

[135] Fr. Gerardo di Flumeri had written an article entitled *"Il richiamo di Padre Pio su Gabriele D'Annunzio"* (The call of Padre Pio on Gabriele D'annunzio) in *Voce di Padre Pio*, May 1997, 16, to which Fr. Pellegrino refers. We quote a few passages. "It was the moment when the poet from

The Padre's commitment

Padre Pio in front of a world which, ignoring or denying God, goes adrift, overwhelmed by compassion for the many brothers who lose faith, must have certainly felt the torment experimented by the apostle Paul who, crying for the loss of his co-nationals, who didn't recognise Jesus as God's Saint, wrote: "I have great heaviness and continual sorrow in my heart" (cf. Rm 9,2).

The urgency he felt to save souls and his need to give all his energy to this task came from this sadness.

The place to do this was always in the confessional.

When he moved to go there, thinking about his task, he was closed in himself, thoughtful, he did not appreciate meeting people or them stopping him. If it happened he answered rapidly. He prayed on his way there.

To those, who seeing him suffering and tired out with work

Abruzzo…was trying to draw inspiration from Franciscanism, desperately trying to get close to the Truth and to the Divine. One day, as if in a state of ecstasy ready to listen to a celestial inspiration, he expressed the wish to meet Padre Pio of Pietrelcina, who at the time was already well-known. We do not know who interceded for him but it is sure that somebody took care of organizing the meeting…

The trip, for unspecified reasons, was cancelled". Mr D'Annunzio had addressed Padre Pio a letter written in his own hand which Fr. Gerardo publishes: *"My dear brother, I know well how many worldly, silly or poisonous tales dim the true fervour of my soul. The fact you have granted me a visit in my retreat and that you have agreed to a brotherly talk with one who has not stopped searching his own inner spirit in a brave way, is a proof of your purity and of your prophet-like insight. Caterina from Siena has taught me how to "enjoy" souls. I already know the value of your soul, Padre Pio. I am sure Francis will smile to us just like when from the unusual grafting he expected an unusual flower and fruit. Ave. Pax et Bonum. Malum et Pax.* The Vittoriale, 28 November 1924. *Gabriele D'Annunzio".*

tried to advise him to rest a little he replied: "I must work. The Confession is firstly a job, then when you don't feel so good it's a sacrifice"[136].

The reply he gave to Fr. Tarcisio Zullo, who begged him to rest a little is astonishing: "How is it possible not to work? Idleness kills me"[137].

But why did he act so intensely and devotedly, heroically more often than not, in a way which we could describe as doggedly?

The Padre often described his mission with the expression: "to wrench souls from Satan". He saw his work as a continuous struggle with the spirit of evil which he had to oppose in every way to pull "his exiled brother" away from its clutches. This fight against evil had been pre-announced to him as a young boy in a vision, before he entered the novitiate of the Capuchins of Morcone in 1903.

A short while before leaving the world and consecrating himself to the Lord, the Saint wrote that he saw "A majestic figure of rare beauty radiant as the sun", who after leading led him to "a vast plain" where there was "a great multitude of people divided into two groups", men of beautiful countenance on one side, dark shadows on the other, he showed him a man of "hideous appearance so tall that his forehead touched the clouds" and he said "it is advisable that you fight this man. Take heart. Enter confidently into the combat, go forward courageously, for I shall be close to you. I will assist you and not allow him to overcome you. I will help you and I won't let him beat you; in reward for the victory over him I'll give you

---

[136] *Personal Diary*: 27 September 1965.
[137] *Chronicle*, 18-24 June 1955, pp. 406-407.

a splendid crown to adorn your head"[138].

In the light of this vision we need to understand what we have said up to now about the apostolic activity of P. Pio: the urgency to carry out that plan that Heaven had shown him, even before he was able to explain his zeal, determination, commitment and haste to act.

Fr. Pellegrino, in the conference we have mentioned, after saying that "a change for the better in Padre Pio's environment was unable not to take place: it was a duty", lets us understand that the penitent in front of this extraordinary confessor that he had chosen, after perhaps coming from afar or after a long wait had to make a precise basic choice: to be with God or Satan. This had to be the aim of his meeting with the Saint.

Our confrère adds: "Padre Pio speaking of a change towards goodness defines it "angelic spirit" of adjustment; and in opposition leaning towards evil is called "diabolic spirit" that which made one be or lean towards the side of demons. And this for the Padre was an apostasy, that is a renunciation to God.

Carlo Campanini

Amongst the examples of conversions, that is true spiritual transformations that took place at San Giovanni Rotondo through the personal work of our Saint, Fr. Pellegrino put that of Carlo Campanini in prime position, "seen not only in its enthusiastic form", but most of all that the decision to follow the Padre brought about practically in the actor's life.

It was known that Carlo was the ideal stooge for Walter Chiari. In fact each time a producer offered a show to the great

---

[138] *Letters I,* p. 1427.

comic Walter, the answer was: "I'll do it as long as you call Campanini as well". Carlo asked to see the script, he read it and if he found even one ambiguous expression he said: "I, as a spiritual son of Padre Pio, can't accept this part".

"In this way, refers our confrère, Carlo Campanini, I won't say he starved but he renounced a lot of earnings.

And I one night explained this to Padre Pio concluding "Padre, let Carlo say a joke or two a bit ambiguous, after all what's an ambiguous phrase if it makes you laugh. Even I have said one sometimes, and it is part of his job".

Padre Pio didn't even answer me. He remained in the same intransigent position with his spiritual son[139].

The path of conversion of Campanini was not easy in fact it was all troubled. He was born in a poor family, brightened by a saint of a mother.

Carlo tells us: "If I have done anything good it is because she, from up there, has prayed for this unfortunate son, who, without her prayers, who knows where he would have ended up". And he remembers that "even if there wasn't any spare cash, if she saw an old lady, she'd bring her to our house, much tour displeasure, because we'd say "There's another plate of pasta that's gone"[140].

The "spark of Padre Pio" was born in him as he says when he was 19. He was working in Argentina with a Piedomont theatre company, that acted in Italian for the emigrants. One

---

[139] Lecture given in San Giovanni Rotondo on 18 April 1985.

[140] The information about Carlo Campanini comes mostly from two lectures given in Biella on 1.12.1986 and in Belluno on 28 March 1984. The first was published by a Prayer Group from the Biella area in a leaflet, in December 1968; the second is on a tape given to us by Fr. Vittorio Mabellini, Capuchin, in Summer 2000.

day, whist he was with a friend, who later became a well known producer, he said: "It was easy to believe in God when one could meet great saints like St. Francis for example, but unfortunately today, there are no longer any great saints".

The person he was speaking to promptly replied: "Well, saints still do exist. We have one in Italy: he's called Padre Pio and he is a Capuchin friar with the wounds of Jesus on his body, and he offers his suffering for the world".

Carlo was struck by these words.

Later he heard talk again of the Saint with stigmata from the Gargano. In 1937 a cousin of his who had joined the Italian voluntary contingent of soldiers sent to Spain to sustain Franco, attributed his return safe and sound to the homeland to the intercession of Padre Pio. His wife as soon as she embraced him said: "Look, if you are here with us it's because I prayed to Padre Pio and I promised I would go and thank him".

The meeting of Campanini with the Padre took place some years later. Carlo himself told this to the Prayer Groups from the Biella area.

"I had the great fortune to meet Padre Pio in 1939. I was disorderly because alas, of the Lord's ten commandments eight were fine with me, but two irritated me; and so I threw them all away and lived like a beast. Perhaps it was my ignorance that stopped Padre Pio from throwing me out when I approached him for the first time on Holy Thursday 1939.

Carlo was in Bari where his company was taking part in a show. As the manager had given not only Friday but also Thursday as days off, he and a friend of his decided to make the most of the occasion to go to meet the Saint of the nearby San Giovanni Rotondo who everyone spoke of.

When they arrived at the Friary, they asked the door-keeper, bro. Gerardo, could they speak to the Padre. The good friar answered: "How on earth do you think you can meet Padre Pio during these days. He suffers all year, imagine how much during the Holy week!".

"But we are artists", said the two, "tied to timesand circumstances that don't depend on us. We can't come back".

They convinced bro. Gerardo and he let them enter the cloister: "All right, wait here".

During the wait the two visitors certainly didn't act as penitent pilgrims: they were still joking as they had done during their journey, when came out Padre Pio.

Says Campanini: "I saw a tall friar; I had the impression to find a giant before me. He came towards us preceded by an odour of phenic acid that shut one's throat and in a reproving tone said: "Even in these days you don't let me pray? What do you want?".

My companion, today a famous producer, said: "We are two poor artists".

"We are all poor; tell me what you want", replied the Saint. Then I, trembling because right from that moment I felt my soul to be naked and I felt an awe that bordered on fear: "Father, we wish to confess".

"Go and prepare yourselves", he answered, "tomorrow morning I will confess you".

But the two artists didn't stop at San Giovanni Rotondo: they had not gone there for that. The meeting had only left in Carlo's soul a great appeal for the Padre.

The actor in giving his testimony with regards to Padre Pio, also speaks about an adventurous journey to San Giovanni Rotondo with a friend in 1946. He said that he heard the Mass celebrated by the Padre and conversed with him during the Holy Sacrifice. "Father, listen, I'm asking you a grace for me and my wife. We are like two gypsies who travel around all year long. We only see our children a few days a year. I haven't studied and I have no educational qualification. Let me stay near my family and my relations".

Carlo says that he also confessed to Padre Pio during this visit of 1946, but in another circumstance he says candidly: "Up till 1950 I had not understood what I needed to understand. My job, our world full of vanity wasn't the most ideal to let me understand Christ's truth. My life, materially speaking was going very well and I owed it to the Padre who had helped me to gain the grace of staying in Rome where I found work in the Cinema and gave me the chance to raise my children and let them get a degree. I owed it all to him. However, although when I was near him I seemed like a trembling sheep is before a butcher, but when I was far away, a voice inside me said: "But is this life…, You are not in a friary!. And I took the wrong road.

At the end of 1949, I had reached the peak of my popularity. I was making three films at the same time, people envied me and said: "Lucky you, surrounded by beautiful women and expensive cars". I'll tell you what I felt in my soul. When I read in the newspaper that someone who was tired of life had killed themselves, I deep inside envied them thinking: "at least you had the courage o get rid of youself". I was in a state in which I hated life".

Campanini gives the reason for this tragic state of affairs. He felt a great emptiness within him: for the double life he was leading, which kept him terrified that they at home would find out" and because he felt "far from God".

A particular circumstance brought Carlo back to the Saint.

He says: "I was living badly because I didn't have inside me a minute of peace or serenity. One evening, not knowing where to go I went towards the "Tre Fontane" (3 Fountains) where Our Lady appeared to Cornacchiola, a communist. It was eleven p.m.. The image of the Mother of Jesus was illuminated and she was looking down to earth. I saw the gaze as a challenge and I said: "What do you want from me?" in me there is only ice but what can I do?".

The day after my wife said to me: "A priest who has escaped from an Eastern Country and has seen some of your films, said if you have no objection, for the jubilee he wants to consecrate the house to the Sacred Heart of Jesus and Mary".

"Objections? None at all, let him do so", I replied.

After an hour the priest arrived and said: "Mr Campanini, the 8th January we will have a big party because we are going to consecrate the house. All must go to Confession and take communion!".

I can't tell you what I went through from that moment. I was like a spectator listening to two voices that spoke to me. One said: "If you go to Confession you will have to change completely, but then what life will you have? The other said: "And if the one on high calls you tonight, where will you go?".

So I started to go round the churches but I chose those where there were long lines of people waiting to confess. Sometimes I said: "Lord, don't let me confess, because you know I'm not ready. I can't do it, I'm not sorry enough. Feeling happy I would go away, but after a while I felt worse than before.

The 6th January arrived; I didn't want to behave falsely at the house blessing, and so I started to make excuses. I told my wife that on that date I had to do some filming outside.

On the morning of the 8th I didn't know what to do. At 9 o'clock I was going around Rome when I found myself in front of St. Anthony's Church in via Merulana. I went in and saw a confessional made of glass, you could see the penitent and the confessor. I said to myself: I'm never going in there. People see me, make a few comments.

In the meantime I watch. Inside was a foreign looking priest with a big ruddy face. He looked like an advert for beer. Inside a voice said to me. "How can you confess to him. He loves life, he loves it more than you". And I didn't take one step.

Whilst I was thinking these thoughts another friar came in the room. I looked up at the Crucifix that moved me and I said: "That's the one I could open my soul to". But what an effort it would take.

I decided finally to go away, but then I saw that priest changed place with the other one. I stopped as if I wasn't interested: before me were at least twenty people.

But the first of the line turned to me and said: "Go ahead sir". So before I realised it I was kneeling down.

I don't know how long I spoke. All I knew was that I was wet through with sweat. After I had been given absolution I asked: "but when can I take communion?".

"When you wish", he answered. I took it immediately.

On 8th January 1950 the priest consecrated the house. I can't tell you how happy my family were when they saw that I too, took communion.

Two days later on 10th January I went by car to Padre Pio. I booked a Confession and waited.

It must be said that when the Padre heard a sin from one's past life he used to say: "No, you have already confessed that". He didn't wish to hear the same Confession twice. So I felt sure I wouldn't be hailed down upon: because I had left the biggest part of my sins in Rome.

My turn arrives. As I was going to open my mouth, Padre Pio said: "Start from 1946". Imagine how I felt.

Whilst I spoke I had my head hung down. He said: "Look at

me, look at me in the face!".

But I couldn't. So the Padre then said: "You are ashamed in front of me who am nobody, but Him above you have offended with no scruples. Your behaviour is cowardice, it's cowardice!". And he pushed me with his knees to move me from the platform to the kneeling stool. He wanted to hear everything. And only after I promised that I would change my lifestyle, he gave me absolution. From that day on, I really started to live.

Mass

The Padre, as well as putting Carlo during his stay at San Giovanni Rotondo, back in God's grace, showed him in those days of conversion the main elements for a new life. As the foundation he put the Eucharist.

Campanini, candidly says that he didn't understand the value neither of Mass nor of Communion, and continued to repeat, as many do, you can be a good Christian without going to Mass.

When he saw the Padre on the altar, stare at the Crucifix or gaze at the consecrated host he said: "But what are those tears and that blood that drips from his hands? What is all this suffering? Why is there such a painful testimony each day before the eyes of all?".

The actor says: "One day as I was thinking about these questions, a clear voice in my heart said these words: "You too look at that Crucifix. Among those spits on his face some are also yours; and that crown of thorns, how many times have you leaned on it to push it harder on his forehead, those hands covered in sores and to those feet, how many hammerings have you also given!".

I burst out sobbing and I would have liked to confess in front of all those in church. I felt a pain I had never felt before in all my life. At the same time I realised I was not hearing a new message, those words reminded me that since I was a child, when I went to catechism, I had been taught that Jesus died for us and that in the Mass his sacrifice was renewed.

But there was still another sign waiting for me.

The morning before my departure I went to the altar to take Communion. When the Padre gave me the host I felt my tongue burn as though someone had put a burning ember on it. It lasted for two hours. My breath had the perfume of bread, like that you can smell when you take homemade bread out of the oven.

I went to hide behind the church, on the side towards the mounting, so no-one could see my tears of joy and emotion. I really felt the Lord's presence. That day to thank Jesus for letting me understand the gift of communion I promised that I would go to Mass and Communion every day.

When I returned to Rome they said I was exaggerating, that my behaviour was close to fanaticism, because the Church itself calls for one Communion a year and Mass on Sundays. But I kept faith to my promise.

As I know my weakness and the art of evil, that when it sees one of its clients like me ripped away, it redoubles temptation. I understood there was only one way to fight it. I called Mass and Communion injections of penicillin against the polio of the soul. As well as this as the body needs to eat two or three times a day to be sustained, I thought my spirit needed daily Communion, especially to live in my working environment.

Faith

The shake up that Campanini received from the Padre in the January of 1950 was for the best and definitely marked his life.

Carlo, speaking of his visit to Padre Pio in 1946, says: "I had received everything from him but I hadn't understood a thing. I had kept my mistaken ideas about faith. I thought that faith was the little stick you put near little plants as they grow: the plants need help or the wind blows them down. Once the plants are grown, the sticks are no longer needed".

The actor thought he could manage his life with good sense without the continuous help from above made from light and strength. He found himself at the mercy of temptation, and as we have seen at the edge of desperation.

This time before leaving San Giovanni Rotondo he wanted to secure himself.

The Padre had said to him: "There are certain films you can't make, especially the films they make nowadays. You must realise that those who make those films will pay before God: from those who put forth the money to the workman who nails just one nail to prepare the scene".

About this subject there was a discussion in the little break the Padre took from his spiritual children. A judge from Florence said to Padre Pio without embarrassment: "Padre, I think you go a bit over the top. Films don't always harm, even those that are X-rated films. I'm seventy years old and I can tell you that films forbidden to those under eighteen years of age have no effect whatsoever on me".

Padre Pio answered: "Ah, they do nothing to you, but the same you can't see them as with the money you pay to watch them you give the opportunity to make these films that can damn souls".

So Campanini, feeling loaded up with responsibility decided to stick to Padre Pio's words and that evening, before returning to Rome asked for his help: "Father, I'm leaving and I will return to that cauldron of Cine-città. I'm afraid, I'm very afraid".

And he: "Good, you should have fear the day you are not afraid. Remember that Satan is like a chained dog. Farther than the chain he cannot go but if you go near him, he will bite you. Remember: stay away from trouble".

Padre Pio, the following morning, when he was saying goodbye, kissed and embraced this son that needed paternal support. Carlo who didn't expect this gesture was over the moon with joy and saw in the Padre's affection a guarantee against future tests.

Once back in Rome, the first difficulties he encountered came from some of his colleagues, those who were the most affectionate and who went to Church. They said to him: "What has work got to do with your behaviour: work is one thing and faith is another. "Carlo defined himself saying: "You can't beat your chest in the morning and in the evening scandalize".

Even at home they wouldn't leave him in peace.

Campanini recounts: "My son, who was about to get his degree , said one day: "Dad, stop going hundreds of kilometres to go and embrace a bearded friar. There are lots in Rome. People will end up thinking you are a bigot. You won't work any more. You know how people in your circle think".

It was inevitable that work started to diminish, not due to others but because of the actor's determination not to accept certain parts.

The economic situation started to become critical. Carlo observes: "Unfortunately taxes arrive after five years and when there are no more takings there are only expenses. These are dreadful moments. However I was never dismayed".

To sustain Campanini in this test like in many others there was only his faith, the "tutor" as he defined it, that is not necessary only for the little plants, but especially.

For the big ones, because there are no trees strong enough to resist a hurricane. And the hurricanes in the life of the spirit are more violent than those which take place in nature.

Love for suffering

Amongst the teachings of Padre Pio the one that struck Carlo the most and that he considers the most important is to do with the love for suffering. One day in Confession the Padre told him: "My son, if humanity could understand the value of suffering, men wouldn't search for pleasure but only pain".

Carlo confesses that at the Saint's word he was aghast: he couldn't understand, but when he became more familiar with the Padre, he grasped the concept.

He said: "Bit by bit, seeing the unheard-of suffering of the Padre, offered with joy for the salvation of our souls, I too began to understand that poor as I was with my suffering I could offer something to Him, master of all".

That teaching however was not only a fundamental truth of Christianity presented to a son who had to make it his spiritual fund but it was to be a clear message.

In fact, shortly after Carlo would have had in the heart of his family a sorrow that would be with him for years. When this thorn made its pain felt he found the strength to support it with dignity and patience remembering the maxim his spiritual father had trusted him with like the viaticum necessary for every day life. And he transformed the test into credit.

"All of us", he says, "have our crosses; I too had one which covered me with shame. I wouldn't have been able to get out of such confusion, if the Padre hadn't enlightened and prepared me. To every offering of my suffering that I made to the Lord he repaid me with a peace and serenity that I never had before".

Heavy going

Carlo to illustrate that his spiritual life was an uphill climb told us of this episode.

He said: "Padre Pio had a great sense of humour. One day he praised my singing: so every time I could I did everything to let him hear me sing. One day after the Padre had recited the "Visit to Sacramented Jesus and Holy Mary" a prayer composed by St. Alfonso M. De Liguori, he bestowed the blessing and soon after the female choir started to sing the hymn dedicated to Our Lady "I'll go and see Her one day".

I was a bit tired but joined in and sang off key in the chorus which begins: "To the Heavens, the Heavens, the Heavens" I wasn't worried though because everybody in the church was singing and it was unlikely that anyone would notice my voice.

When the service was over the Padre went back in the sacristy and I went in too together with the men who observed the rule of silence. After a while the Saint looked at me and said "Hey you, when it comes to getting to heaven you always have a bit of a struggle don't you?".

Everybody laughed. I laughed too….to join in the fun; but I knew that the Padre wasn't only joking".

An anonymous… but touching conversion

We have known so many souls who have returned to God after being helped by the Padre to make a real conversion! Of the many we wish to remember only one who struck us for the determination with which she changed her lifestyle, to give herself completely to God.

D.P. was a war widow. After the death of her husband, her in-laws took no notice of her or of her two children, nor did they offer to help them in any way. On the contrary, when during the Second World War, she and the children moved from the town into the country where they could have survived, the in-laws had stripped the house and taken everything away. D., whose eldest son was to make his first Communion, didn't even manage to receive back from them one of her husband's suits to remodel to fit the boy.

After a year or two, in order to support the family, she was forced to work at the "Michelin" factory where she had already worked before getting married. Since she lived and since she was in financial difficulties, she rightly asked her in-laws to give her back the house which had been assigned to their son. But her efforts were vain.

She needed advice about what to do and thought about going to see Padre Pio, but she hadn't got enough money to pay for the three of them to make such a long journey. She decided to gamble on the Lottery. She went to the betting office and said to those working there, "Help me to win, I beg you because I really need to win". They just laughed at her ,but she insisted and so they, after asking her questions about her life advised her to play three numbers:2-18-50.

One Monday she played the numbers on the Florence lottery wheel: the following Saturday she read in the newspaper that her numbers had come up. She had won 86,000 lire: which in 1953 was a large sum. "With that money you could buy something useful for the house, instead of just going to San Giovanni Rotondo", her brother said. And so she did.

Her eldest son protested at length. He said to her: "Mum, you are a liar, I don't believe you any more".

After a while the poor woman thought about gambling again and said: "If Padre Pio helps me, we will go to San Giovanni Rotondo". She won 25,000 lire. She bought a dress for herself and new trousers for the boys and off they went.

When they arrived they lodged in somebody's house who let them sleep in a corridor. They stayed in San Giovanni Rotondo for 14 days waiting to go to Confession.

D. was struck by the Mass celebrated by Padre Pio. She tells us: "I saw Padre Pio in direct contact with God. His hands bled and I am sure he re-lived the scene that took place on Calvary before Our Lady". So every morning at 4.00 a.m she was waiting for the church doors to open. It was there, in front of the altar where the Saint celebrated Mass, that her soul was illuminated.

She was living with a man she adored but decided to end the relationship and tell all to Padre Pio. When her turn came she approached the confessional trembling. She was so nervous she hardly knew what she was doing. She only said: "What can I do to live as I have done recently? I want to make a full Confession".

Padre Pio: "Are you truly sorry for your past sins?".

"That's why I am here. I want to change. I want to live as I have lived the last few days".

And the Padre "Well then go in peace with God. Now come here in front".

She obeyed going in front of the confessional. The Saint after a brief examination of conscience gave her absolution and placed his wounded hands on her head for quite a while.

Before going away D. asked once more: "At home what shall I do to live as I have done here?

Padre Pio "In your town you will find someone who will help you"[141].

When she went home after a week she met Ida Dalla Piccola who was the sister of the notary who was with Chiara Lubich, the founded the Focolarini movement. D. entered the movement and her life changed.

She convinced the man she was living with to marry the girl who had given him a daughter. In the factory where she had sometimes used bad language she said to her friends: "I apologise if during break-time I have shocked you with my dirty jokes. You won't hear me tell them any more". She stopped feeling bitter and wanting revenge against her in-laws even though they had received 54 millions (Italian Lira) for the house in her husband's name for war damage, whilst she had received no benefits whatsoever.

She decided not to marry again, also because one of her sons suffered from ill-health. She lived by working and with the help of her husband's war pension which arrived 6 years after his death. Padre Pio protected her sons and cured the one who was ill[142].

---

[141] Actually Padre Pio gave the name of the town where the penitent lived even though she had not mentioned it during Confession.

[142] Testimony taken at Baselga di Pinè (TN) 24.10.1998.

II. SINS AS SEEN BY PADRE PIO

The Padre in Confession when listening to a transgression admitted by a penitent usually repeated: "It's a sin, it's a sin!".

Often we tend to regulate our actions or even justify our mistakes through human motives and reasons. If they do not refer to the Word of God which gives precise rules of behaviour, they cannot bring us to perfect morality or let us be sure we will not make mistakes.

With regards to the need to follow a moral law dictated by God to guide us in our doings, Edith Stein, St. Teresa Benedicta of the Cross writes: "Those who believe in God know that there is One whose sight is not limited by the horizon. One who embraces and permeates everything. Who lives in the certainty of this faith, feels in his conscience he can no longer be satisfied with his own science, no matter how vast it may be. He must necessarily strive to get to know what is right before God's eyes. This is the reason why only a behaviour based on religiousness can really be an ethical conduct. Of course there is a research of and a natural tendency towards what's right and what's good and, in some cases, one may even be able to find it, but only in the research for the divine will one can really achieve the goal"[1].

---

[1]   EDITH STEIN St. Teresa Benedicta of the Cross, *Incontro a Dio, antologia di scritti spirituali*, edited by Maria Cecilia del Volto Santo, Ed Paoline, 1998, 76.

Padre Pio always searched to know God's will and do it, that is to put it in action whatever the cost or sacrifice. Fr. Pellegrino who confirmed that Padre Pio's main worry was "the feverish research for God's will", gives us an account which is worth looking at. One day the Saint, after the ladies' Confession, was returning into the Friary and he saw a child who was crying in the middle of the men who were waiting for him to pass by in the corridor. "Why are you crying?" he asked".

I tore my trousers whilst I was playing and my dad told me off", answered the little boy". "Eh, who knows how many trousers we tore when we were children!" said Padre Pio.

A few minutes later Fr. Pellegrino who was accompanying the Padre jokingly said: "Father, so when you were a boy, you were naughty and ripped your trousers a lot".

The Padre said: "I personally have never torn any trousers. I said that just to let the boy stop crying".

Then he added: "my face, yes I would always tear it to do God's will"[2].

God's will was a fixed reference point for the direction of souls for Padre Pio. Often, because of his reactions to the transgressions of God's laws, those who were close to him would have preferred him to take a softer line which would have been more understandable to others.

Even Fr. Pellegrino marvelled at this strictness when the Saint denounced the sin of abortion. Padre Pio justified this need to speak clearly to God's people, who are often left to themselves: "Do you know what the trouble is? Those who come to church not needing to clear their thoughts are filled up with good words and superficial advice, whilst those who

---

[2]   A conference held on 18-4-85. see also page 74.

need to be shown some light leave without anything for their salvation. Brotherly strictness is worth more than all the sugariness of the world put together"[3].

1. Abortion: A sin against life

We wish to make a little review of sins as Padre Pio "saw" them starting with abortion, which today many do not feel is unjust or wicked. The Church teaches: "Human Life must be respected and protected absolutely from the moment of conception. From the first moment of his existence, a human being must be recognised as having the rights of a person, among which is the inviolable right of every innocent being to life"[4].

Many considering this sin confuse State Law, which allows the termination of a pregnancy, with God's Law, for which abortion remains a sin against the fifth commandment "Do not kill."(Es 20.13 Mt 5-21-22) which defends life whatever the number of years, months or days of a human being.

A terminated pregnancy is always a trauma, a drama, and it cannot be denied that what the woman, who unfortunately does not wish to be a mother, does, involves all those around her, including the strongly emotive participation and sometimes justification of a choice which is so mistaken. Confessors know of this involvement, even if they can never justify the suppression of a life.

Fr. Pellegrino one day said to our Saint: "Father, this morning you denied absolution to a woman who had had an abor-

---

[3] Pellegrino Funicelli *Il rigore vale più delle sdolcinature* in *Voce di Padre Pio,* December 1976, 12.

[4] *Catechismo della Chiesa Cattolica*, Libreria Editrice Vaticana, 1993, n. 2270.

tion. Why were you so severe with the poor wretch?".

Padre Pio answered. "The day in which men, because they are afraid of the economic boom, physical damage, or economic sacrifices, lose the horror of abortion, will be a terrible day for humanity. Because that will really be the day, that they should be horrified".

Then, gripping the speaker's gown with his right hand he put his left hand to his breast as if he wished to control his heart and continued in a peremptory way: "Abortion is not only homicide but also suicide. Do we want to save those we see on the brink of committing both crimes with one blow or not?!".

"Why suicide?", asked Fr. Pellegrino.

"Assailed by one of those not unusual divine furies counteracted by an endless background of sweetness and goodness", Padre Pio answered: "You would understand this suicide of the human race if you could see using your brain the "beauty and joy" of the earth, populated only by old people and depopulated of children: burnt like a desert.

If you reflected, you would understand the double gravity of abortion: with abortion the life of the parents is also mutilated. I'd like to cover these parents with the ashes of their destroyed children, to nail them to their responsibility and deny them the possibility of claiming their ignorance: The remains of a procured abortion should not be burned with false care and pity. It would be a terrible hypocrisy. Those ashes should be thrown in the face of those hard faced murderous parents. Leaving them in Good Faith would make me feel involved in their crime. I am sure God approves of my strictness, because from Him after this painful battle against evil, I always gain, in fact I feel a sensation of wonderful calm for a quarter of an hour".

Fr. Pellegrino objected that "if it is impossible to destroy the obsessive fixation from the mind of the person who was to abort, it was useless to treat them so severely and badly according to the rigour of the Church", Padre Pio said: "My strictness in defending the arrival of children to the world is always an act of faith and of hope for our meeting with God on earth. Unfortunately, as time goes by, the battle becomes stronger than our forces, but it must be fought the same, because from the certainty of our defeat on paper our battle draws the guarantee of the real victory; that of the new earth and new Heavens"[5].

What reasons or justifications of this sin can one oppose this consideration?

According to the Church "formal co-operation in abortion constitutes a grave offence"[6].

In the sacristy in front of the confessional, where Padre Pio listened to the penitents, Mario Tentori waited his turn sitting on the bench. Whilst he was examining his conscience he heard the Padre shout: "Get out you animal!, go away!" The Saint's words were addressed to a man who had just knelt down to confess and had come out humiliated, upset and confused.

The day after Mario took the train from Foggia to return to Milan. He sat down in a compartment in which there was only one other traveller. This person started to look at him closely and made it clear he wanted to start a conversation. Finally he asked: "Weren't you at San Giovanni Rotondo yesterday, in the sacristy to confess to Padre Pio?".

---

[5]   P. Pellegrino Funicelli, *Il rigore fraterno* in *Voce di Padre Pio*, December 1976 11-12.

[6]   Catechismo…, n.2272.

"Yes I was" answered Tentori.

The other continued "We were sitting on the same bench, and I went in before you. I'm the one Padre Pio threw out calling me "animal". Do you remember?".

"Yes, I do", answered Mario once more.

The traveller continued: "You others around the confessional didn't hear the words that made Padre Pio send me away. Well then, Padre Pio said word for word "Get out animal, get away because in agreement with your wife you have aborted three times". Now do you understand? The Padre said "You have aborted! Yes meaning me, because the idea of my wife having an abortion was always mine".

He then burst out sobbing which expressed as he admitted his pain and his will not to sin again and his strong determination to return to Padre Pio to receive absolution and change his life style[7].

Padre Pio's strictness had saved the life of a father who after denying life to three children was running the risk of losing his soul for eternity.

2. Non-fulfilment of marital vows

The fall in births, which are often programmed for egoistic reasons or economic worries is depopulating the earth, as the Saint says, "burnt like a desert", because it is without the smiles of children. This ageing of the earth is also influenced by apprehensions of a medical nature.

A spiritual son confided to us: "In the second Confession I had with him, in the first he sent me away, when I finished

---

[7]   Don Bruno Borelli, Erba 19.9.1998.

my Confession the Padre asked me: "Is there anything else? I answered no.

He looked me closely in the eyes and asked "have you done things for the good of Holy matrimony with your wife?".

"No, Father", I answered, "Because doctors have forbidden us to have other children".

He said wanting clarification: "What have the doctors to do with these things!?".

They said that we could give birth to a monster. "I answered.

"And this is what you would have deserved" the Saint shouted and once more sent me away from the confessional"[8].

The thing is that, in this changing world, matrimony is losing its sacredness, since it is managed by man for his liking. The Padre however remains true to the Law of God, man's creator, to whom he gave rules to have him as his collaborator to continue human life on earth.

Sister Vincenza Tremigliozzi, Mother Superior of the "San Giuseppe" Hostel in San Giovanni Rotondo recounts "Padre Pio did not give absolution to a lady who was staying with us. When I saw she was so distressed and downhearted I went to see the Padre and said "Father that woman is crying".

"And did she tell you why I didn't give her absolution?".

"Yes because she doesn't want children".

And the Saint with a determined and severe tone said "You must tell her she is trampling on God's Sacraments".

The Sister was so moved that she clasped her hands to her breast[9].

---

[8]   Testimony taken at San Giovanni Rotondo 27.9.1994.

[9]   Sr. Vincenza Tremigliozzi, S. Giovanni Rotondo 16.5.1999.

Another testimony is even more moving. One day a woman left the Friary to go to her hotel, Villa Maria, she was sobbing her heart out. To those who asked her what had upset and pained her so much, she was unable to say a word. When she finally calmed down she said, still with tears in her eyes. "Padre Pio sent me away from Confession because I said my husband didn't want children. He shouted: "He will get cancer!" And to the people who tried to console her she added with terror in her eyes "My husband already has cancer, he already has it"[10].

Engagement

Too often before marriage the future newly-weds prepare everything except the base to ensure the strength of their union. The Catechism of the Catholic Church says:

So that the "I do" of the spouses may be a free and responsible act, and so that the marriage covenant may have solid and lasting human and Christian foundations, preparation for marriage is of prime importance" (n.1632). The Italian Bishops remind us that " focusing on the choice of faith and basic moral values" must be part of "the principal contents of the engagement, a most special time[11].

A marriage that was not based on God was inconceivable for Padre Pio.

One day at San Giovanni Rotondo, a woman and her young daughter approached me and asked me to be a go-between

---

[10]   *Notes... San Giovanni Rotondo* May 1993.
[11]   *La verità vi farà liberi..., n.*1083.

with Padre Pio to find out what he thought about a problem that was worrying them.

They had come down from Trento and had booked to confess to Padre Pio. They wished to ask for some important advice The girl was engaged to a young man who was a member of a secular party and acted and declared himself to be a non-believer: The girl who had been brought up a Catholic and practised her faith didn't know what to do, she wondered if she should break off her engagement or not. Unfortunately the time they had to wait for Confession was longer than they had expected and they could no longer stay on the Gargano but reluctantly had to return home. They did not wish to do so without receiving some enlightening advice from Padre Pio with regards to this worrying problem.

So the mother asked me to speak to the Padre and I did so that same day. I told him the problem. The Saint after listening to me said: "And on what do they wish to base their marriage if they remove God?".

His answer was clear and precise but I, thinking of the two women who wanted some practical advice, said to the Padre: "What should the young girl do about her fiancée?".

He after looking at me a little surprised at my insistence at asking another question, almost as if I hadn't understood him said shortly: "Send him to you know where!".

I went to the cloisters at the fixed time and told the women Padre Pio's words, which needed no further explanation. They thanked me and left.

A week later, I was giving a hand to the brothers who dealt with the correspondence and as I opened an envelope a photo of a young girl fell out onto the desk. I was surprised as it seemed to be a face I knew; in fact it was the girl from Trento I had helped by giving her the Padre's thoughts about her future marriage. She still needed a word from the Saint. She wrote that when her boyfriend heard the words of Padre Pio, she heard him say that he did believe in God and that only he knew his own inner thoughts.

As the letter, which was addressed to Padre Pio, mentioned my name, I felt it my duty to return to the Padre to once more discuss the case. The Saint who distinguished himself by his meekness and patience, listened to me but he ended the conversation with a few words: "Padre Pio only speaks once".

The truth that he had expressed a few days before did not need to be altered, the Padre had spoken drawing from the light of God.

Fr. Marcello Lepore, offers us a testimony which has the same flavour as the previous one.

A girl went to speak to Padre Pio, she said: "Father I don't get on with my boyfriend. He isn't religious and he doesn't believe in God. I wish to leave him, but he has told me that if I leave him he will throw himself down the well".

To which the Padre replied "He's already in the well and he can't go any deeper"[12].

Preparing for matrimony

The Italian Bishops whom we have referred to, add to the above quote: "The aim of an engagement is not that of testing love by having premarital sexual relationships".

However we must realise that today's young people are children of a new morality and feel certain moral values are out-dated. The Document of the Italian Episcopal Conference

---

[12]   Fr. Marcello Lepore, Foggia 21.12.1998.

says: "The culture of love that has established itself in the west has some positive aspects: personal freedom, equal rights for men and women the integration of their different personal qualities responsible procreation. It tends however to reduce love to individual satisfaction through the possession of each other; it allows sex out of marriage; it wishes homosexuality to be accepted; it separates love from procreation and all rules, except hygienic ones and those against violence"[13].

Many testimonies tell us of the care the Padre took in order to enlighten, through his advice and reproaches, young people who were planning to get married. This for Padre Pio was to be included in God's plan for each of his children. He did not therefore approve of the haste of some people to find a soul mate at all costs.

The Saint said to Lucietta Pennelli: "You have to get it into your mind that the Lord loves you more than you love yourself. If He wants you to get married, He knows where you live and He will come and look for you". He also told her that listening to her parents would not go a miss but would actually help her.

This spiritual daughter of his tells us "I was keen on a boy, but my family were quite against this relationship. Padre Pio instead was on my side. One day my fiancée, seeing that my family did not approve of him, suggested that we elope, that was the custom used at the time by lots of young people to resolve the problem, but it was also the start of them living in sin. From that day forwards I didn't answer his letters anymore.

When my turn to confess came, after I had finished con-

---

[13] *La verità vi farà liberi…, n.* 1043.

fessing I said: "Father, I want to finish with Domenico". But I didn't mention his proposition.

Padre Pio who had left me to make a free choice said: "I was waiting for this". Then he added: "More often than not God's will is shown to us by the will of superiors, in your case your parents. So we can say the relationship was not the will of God."

The Padre, who naturally did not allow passionate premarital relationships warned: "Go slowly, don't do things so that, if the Lord hasn't made you one for the other, you will not suffer later".

Sacred words of thought for young people![14].

The element that Padre Pio put in prime position for the preparation of the Sacrament with which a man and a woman are indissolubly joined together was prayer.

When Probo Vaccarini returned home from the Second World War, he expressed in Confession his difficulty in finding a girl with serious intentions to settle down with. Padre Pio advised him to seek help from the Heavenly Virgin. On seeing the expression of disbelief on the penitent's face the Padre added: "What do you think Our Lady doesn't know how to choose the right girl for you? Pray I said"[15].

Padre Pio had grave doubts about young people meeting in places such as ballrooms or the like where everything except a persons spirituality is shown.

A young man from Milan, Rinaldo Campidoglio, a spiritual son of Padre Pio, came one day to San Giovanni Rotondo and

---

[14]   Lucietta Pennelli, San Giovanni Rotondo 7.12.1995.
[15]   See p. 39, note 42.

in my presence said to the Saint: "Father I have met a girl and I'd like to get engaged". Naturally enough the news was given to see what Padre Pio thought, as this was important for his spiritual children.

The Padre asked: "Where did you meet her?".

"At the seaside", answered Rinaldo.

And Padre Pio: "Devil's work!" so ended the dialogue and the young man's contact with the girl.

It is almost futile to say that Padre Pio wanted his spiritual children or those who said they were his friends to be chaste. Once they told him, one of his affectionate admirers was getting married because his girlfriend was expecting. They asked if he were to bless their wedding. Padre Pio was almost surprised by this request and answered "Ah, yes now you even want me to give him a prize!"[16].

Divorce and the Family

The break-up of a marriage through divorce made the Saint's fatherly heart suffer terribly. He was violently against divorce and said "Divorce is the passport to Hell". He gave so much importance to the family that he could not let it drown so easily!

In the united Holy Family Padre Pio saw the place where faith grows. Most of all he wanted babies to be baptised within three days, so that the little one's heart would quickly become God's dwelling place[17].

---

[16] *Notes...San Giovanni Rotondo*, May 1993.
[17] Umberto Di Girolamo, Trapani 28.10.1996.

"Following the laws of nature the first words a baby speaks are mamma and papa", he said, "then the names of Jesus and Mary should follow". So it is in the family that the dialogue with the spiritual world begins. To those who asked him which prayers they should say daily he answered: "Those that your mother taught you".

The Saint saw in mothers and fathers, the teachers and tutors of morality to be transmitted to their children by example and word. To one who asked him a practical method of living a good Christian life he answered: "As your parents taught you to do". For this reason the Padre was against the idea of boarding schools. He asserted that the children "If they had anything good in them lost it and were influenced by the wickedness of others".[18]

---

[18]   Pietro Cugino, San Giovanni Rotondo 13 May 1993.

Pietro was born in San Giovanni Rotondo 29 June 1913. He met Padre Pio as a child when he went with his blind father to the Friary. At the age of 12 he too became blind and the Saint took him under his wing. His mother wanted to put him in boarding school to give him the chance to learn something that could be useful to him later on in life, but when she told the Saint of her intention and her worries for her son's future, she found the Padre completely against this idea. "You'll lose him there", he said, "He has to stay here. As long as there is Padre Pio he won't go without anything". When he was 4 years old the Padre let him become a tertiary Franciscan and bit by bit he worked for the Friary as a helper: in the morning carrying the shopping that Aunt Rachelina Russo the friar's procurator gave him or by going to the post office to collect the incoming post and deliver the outgoing post. At midday he ate in the Friary and in the evening, if there was bad weather, he had a room for the night. Often he accompanied Padre Pio when he went up again to the Friary. The Padre said: "I give you my eyes and you give me your arm". Padre Pio needed supporting because he often had dizzy spells. Every morning Pietro was next to the altar where the Saint celebrated Holy Mass. Some spiritual children observed that whilst he obtained many cures for those who came from far away, he left Pietro in

One day Marco, the son of Dr. Sala, Padre Pio's personal doctor went to the Friary to complain. He told Padre Pio: "My dad wants to send me to boarding school and I don't want to go".

"Send him to me", promptly replied the Padre.

The day after the doctor met Padre Pio who said to him: "Listen, why do you want to send that poor boy to boarding school?".

"Father, you know how many children I have at home, five and they are all lively and they drive everybody crazy, from their mother to the house-keeper.

"And have you forgotten what you were like? Did your parents put you in boarding school?".

After these words Marco wasn't sent away[19].

If the Padre put prayer in prime position for the preparation of a marriage that would last in time, he also considered the dialogue with God a true safe guard of the Holy Union.

A young married woman confessed to him in 1962. At the end of her Confession the Padre gave her a penitence and then said: "You must enclose yourself in the silence of prayer and you'll save your marriage".

She was most surprised at these words from the Saint as everything at home seemed to be going smoothly. However the storm broke and she was not unprepared. Remembering the Padre's words she turned to prayer and faced the test. With

---

his blindness. One day Pietro went to say hello to Padre Pio and Michele Fini mentioned this fact. The Saint as if to end the discussion once and for all turned to Pietro and said "Pietro but do you want your sight or not? The humble blind boy replied "Father you often say to me "Lucky you Pietro who can't see the ugliness in this world. Now then if I have to see again but risk losing my soul I prefer to stay as I am".

[19] Mariangela Casu, Oristano 21.4.1999.

the strength drawn from God she managed to save her family from a sure break-up[20].

3. Disobeying the sixth commandment

The Italian Bishops considering what St. Paul wrote to the Christians of Thessalonians *"Each of you must learn to control his body as something holy and held in honour not yielding to the promptings of passion as the heathens do in their ignorance of God."* (1 Tess 4-4-5), after giving wise advice to young people about the need to educate their own sexuality observe: "Unfortunately many young people lose their faith because they are unable to remain chaste"[21].

It is to be noted that, according to Spiritual Masters, there are sins that put out the light of faith in a particular way and remove one from heavenly reality amongst these sins they put impurity or lust.

St. Thomas Aquinas states: "The sins of impure pleasure are those which cause the dissolution of the soul"[22].

St. Alfonso M. de Liguori asserts "You go to Hell because of this sin or also with it".

Padre Pio followed the line of thought of these two great doctors of the Church.

In 1968, to a priest who in Confession, confessed he had difficulty in keeping chaste the Saint putting him on guard against possible transgressions said: "Lust is the shortest and

---

[20]   Francesca De Donatis, Taranto 31.5.1999.

[21]   *La verità… n. 1082.*

[22]   G. DAL SASSO – R. COGGI: *Compendio della Somma Teologica di San Tommaso d'Aquino,* Edizioni Studio Domenicano, Bologna 1989, 300.

easiest way to go to Hell. You know this and you say it to others. Try to practise what you preach"[23].

Impurity "is the shortest and easiest way that leads to eternal death, because it "removes the pleasure of prayer, weakens
faith until it extinguishes it. It allows all sins to make the heart
hard and without any particular grace dragging it to the final
un-repentance. According to the book of Apocalypse, fornica-
tion is idolatry (cfr.2-3).

If sin against the sixth and ninth commandment is the cause
of spiritual ruin for all, it is especially for those who have decided to follow Jesus in priesthood or the religious life by being poor, humble and chaste. For Padre Pio the danger of the
failure of everyone who has been consecrated to God is due
to this vice. The Saint said to a priest: "Impurity is the rock
against which many vocations are shattered".

Therefore he was severe with those who had taken their
vows and gave in, without fighting with all their force against
the temptations which are before all.

One day Brother Gerardo, the door keeper of the Friary at
San Giovanni Rotondo went from the sacristy to the Friary
looking for a confessor. He knocked at the cell door of Father
Federico Carrozza and he asked him to confess a young ecclesiastic who was waiting in the waiting room. The priest arrived
after a minute or two, but quickly realised that the penitent was
very troubled.

As soon as the man started to speak his anxiety turned into
indignation. He was almost furious because as soon as he had
approached the confessional Padre Pio had sent him away before he could even open his mouth. However he still wished
to confess.

---

[23]   Testimony given in San Giovanni Rotondo on 21.12.1996.

After making the sign of the cross and the opening prayers the young man pulled a note out of his pocket. On it were written his sins: those against the sixth commandment were quite grave.

After listening the confessor asked "Did Padre Pio read these sins?" and the penitent replied that he hadn't.

"Well then "added the wise friar, "Don't you think that it was God himself who sent you away, directing Padre Pio's actions through supernatural enlightenment? Otherwise you must think that whoever denied you the comfort of the Sacrament without reason must be a madman".

At these words the young man burst into tears and after receiving absolution, found peace in his spirit once more[24].

Indecent entertainment

The Padre was saddened by the scandal that comes from in the indecent entertainment offered to the public by the mass-media.

The Church which has always called our attention to chastity, speaking of the relatively new phenomena of pornography, which even Christians are dangerously becoming accustomed to, says: "Pornography consists in removing real or simulated sexual acts from the intimacy of the partners, in order to display them deliberately to third parties. It offends chastity because it perverts the conjugal act, the intimate giving of spouses to each other. It does grave injury to the dignity of its participants. (Actors, vendors , the public) since each becomes an object of base pleasure and illicit profit for others. It im-

---

[24]   P. Federico Carrozza, Venafro (CB) June 1986.

merses all who are involved in the illusion of a fantasy world. It is a grave offence"[25].

We have seen that with regards to the planning and making of scandalous films, Padre Pio one day said to Carlo Campanini "Those who have only nailed one nail to make the film are also responsible. God will ask them to pay the price". The actor repeated the Padre's words every time he was invited to speak about his conversion[26].

Padre Pio was not keen on television, on the contrary he worried about it, because he thought it could become a means of scandalous images or harmful messages coming into the intimacy of our homes.

We know that the spiritual children always asked the Padre his opinion before doing anything. We have learnt from more than one that when this means of communication began to spread, the Saint did not give everyone the permission to buy a television. His approval was conditioned by the maturity of the user-to-be.

We must note that with regards to shows the Padre went even further. He didn't consider them exactly suitable for those who really wished to live a spiritual life. In the Saint's opinion entertainment even if it was not sinful "was inadmissible" because it could be a moment of distraction from leaning towards perfection.

To some spiritual daughters who had asked permission to go to Foggia to see a religious film he said "Certainly it is a good thing, but you would lose a lot of time that could be spent in prayer."

What would the Padre say about the waste of time spent by many Christians, using the television badly?

---

[25] *Catechismo…*, n. 2354.

[26] Anna Baroni, Chiavari 8.12.1994.

Dancing: an opportunity to sin

The Christian is to avoid sin, as he promises in the act of repentance before receiving absolution for his sins from the priest in confession. Padre Pio like every other good confessor warned his penitents not to be the cause of temptation for others, even if they had no clear or determined intention to cause harm.

We have a testimony that clearly illustrates the Padre's thoughts. Lucietta Pennelli who has already mentioned precious advice she received from the Saint, tells us: "I loved dancing. I was a dragonfly. Dancing with a man or a woman, twisting or jumping around a chair, it was all the same to me. Naturally this took place at home with neighbours or relatives and my parents watching what was going on. However the Padre did not approve.

One day in Confession, after confessing I had danced he said: "If you dance again, I'll send you away".

After a while however there was a wedding and I against my will, found myself dancing. For fear that the Padre would throw me out as I approached the confessional I went to confess to another priest, who didn't make any comment about my dancing and asked if there was anything else. As I had nothing else to say he gave me absolution I went home but I was not at peace.

The day after I went to confess to the Padre who at the sound of my voice said "Well then have you changed your confession day?".

I told him everything and finished saying "I was afraid you would send me away".

He remained for a while in silence and then said: "You really want a good hiding, don't you?".

I didn't answer and he said "I won't send you away but don't do it again".

Then I said "Father I assure you that when I dance I don't think about anything, I'm just careful not to step on the toes of whoever is dancing with me!".

Padre Pio said "You can be sure of your feelings but not those of others. I don't condemn dancing as such, but I believe there is always the danger of sin and the Holy Spirit says: "He who puts himself in danger, perishes in it" (sir 3,27)[27].

Indecent fashion: another occasion of sin

Padre Pio had nothing against people taking care of their appearance. In the morning after washing before going down to church to celebrate Holy Mass, he combed his hair and tidied his ruffled beard. He, who believed in Holy poverty, often wore his habit which had been patched or darned, but he always wanted it to be clean.

Order, cleanliness, and dignity were the qualities he wanted in the way his spiritual children dressed. Enzo Bertani who for along time was one of the managers of The Home for the Relief of Suffering tells us: "I needed a new suit and being a member of the Franciscan Third Order, I didn't want to spend a lot. Before going shopping I said to our spiritual father "Father I wish to spend less on my clothes".

Padre Pio answered "in your position you have to dress decorously. You must have no scruples about that"[28].

In a similar situation, when Enzo wanted to save money

---

27 Lucietta Pennelli, San Giovanni Rotondo 7.12.1995.
28 Enzo Bertani, San Giovanni Rotondo 21.1.1995.

when buying a pair of shoes, the Padre said, "Get a good pair, then they will last longer"[29].

Mrs Rina Giostrelli, who married Count Telfener who had been chosen by the Padre as one of his collaborators in the making of his great hospital affirms: "During the last World War there was no chance of buying wool or thread to make socks, so we undid lace and with the thread from the lace we made slippers and little shoes".

One day Padre Pio saw I had these things on my feet and he said: "You must go about dressed in a dignified way: you have to do so for your husband's sake. If I wore a torn habit I wouldn't make a good impression of St. Francis"[30].

When a girl who dressed in a scruffy way went to moan to the Saint because she couldn't find a husband, the Padre seeing her so miserable, burst out: "Daughter of mine, smarten yourself up a bit!"[31].

The Padre, who always expressed a balanced point of view, wished that his spiritual children showed good sense in the way they dressed.

Mrs Rina Giostrelli continues: "When I first moved with my husband to San Giovanni Rotondo I used to wear a hat. Padre Pio, when he saw me for the first time, looked at me with an ironic smile. This took place two or three times; then seeing that I had not understood, one day he said: "But do you think you are prettier with that thing on your head?". I stopped wearing it immediately[32].

The Padre helped her understand it was one thing to go to the

---

[29] Enzo Bertani, San Giovanni Rotondo 4.12.1995.
[30] Countess Telfener, San Giovanni Rotondo 6.5.1993.
[31] GHERARDO LEONE, *Giorni di quaresima nello spirito di Padre Pio,* in *La Casa Sollievo della Sofferenza*, Year LIV n. 5-6 (1-31 March 2003), 5.
[32] Countess Telfener, San Giovanni Rotondo, 6.5.1993.

theatre and another to go around the Friary or be in church.

Another time he was much severer. To a woman who was wearing a hat with a long feather and who was waiting near his confessional Padre Pio said: "You, go and confess to the devil". We don't know if the Saint had read more in that soul. Probably he had[33].

Most of all it was modesty in the way of dressing that was most dear to the Padre's heart, no matter where one lived. The reason that the Saint worried was that an indecent way of dressing can be scandalous and an occasion of sin for anyone.

Scandal, says the catechism, "is an attitude or behaviour which leads another to do evil. The person who gives scandal becomes his neighbour's tempter. He damages virtue and integrity; he may even draw his brother into spiritual death. Scandal is a grave offence if by deed or omission another is deliberately led into grave offence" (n. 2284). And it is to be noted that the same sin is committed even when one does not deliberately have bad intentions.

Jesus says *"But I tell you that he who casts his eye on a woman so as to lust after her has already committed adultery with her in his heart"*(Mt 5,28).

Certainly the sin is to be attributed to the malice of man but woman can be culpable because it is she who gives the incentive and excuse for sin.

Scandal is a word that comes from Greek and means "difficulty", "obstacle". It is like a stick that one throws between a man's feet when he is running; he trips and falls.

Spiritual death can arrive through the eyes!

Once the Saint looked out of the window to greet the peo-

---

[33]   *Notes...*, San Giovanni Rotondo, May 1993.

ple gathered on the field in front of his little bedroom window. From a loudspeaker which spread his voice the words "How much immodesty there is in the way you are dressed. You should be ashamed of yourselves"[34].

The Padre continually appealed to women to be modest in their way of dressing. His spiritual daughters say he had announced a crusade against indecent fashion. The reason was always the same: a certain way of dressing could be scandalous.

Padre Pio said one day to Mrs Emilia Sanguinetti, the wife of Dr. Sanguinetti who was the main collaborator in the building of the "Home for the Relief of Suffering": "I wish my spiritual children to begin a holy battle against these immodest fashions, if they wish me to help them in their troubles"[35].

And the Padre never missed a chance to make his reproaches.

To a lady, the wife of a consul, who was introduced to him by Fr. Carmelo of Sessano, the Saint on seeing her bare arms said: "I would cut your arms off, so you would suffer much less than you will suffer in Purgatory"[36].

On an other occasion he said: "Bare skins will burn".

One day he sent one of his spiritual daughters to tell a woman who was sitting in church with her legs crossed, to sit properly[37].

He didn't make the slightest allowance for the dress code of his spiritual daughters. Lucietta Pennelli says: "one day I went to church in a beautiful new dress that was slightly low-cut due not to a style created by the dressmaker but to a cut mistake.

---

[34]   Anna Baroni, Chiavari 8.12.1994.
[35]   *Notes…,* May 1993.
[36]   P. Carmelo Durante, Larino Summer 1986.
[37]   *Notes…,* May 1993.

Padre Pio saw me in church and asked: "Who made you that dress?".

"Graziella Cascavilla", I answered. She too was a spiritual daughter of the Padre.

"Don't wear it again" said the Padre.

I didn't want to throw it away so I had the idea of covering the low-cut neckline with a scarf. On Sunday I went to listen to the Padre's Mass and he also gave me Communion; but once out of church a teacher from San Severo, Giulia De Julio told me: "This morning whilst giving you the host, Padre Pio looked at you insistently".

I understood. A few days later I went to confess. The Padre as soon as he opened the grate said: "Do you really think you can fool me?".

"Father, what do you mean?", I answered.

"With that rainbow wrapped round your neck you don't cover a thing. I told you not to wear that dress again!".

"But Father, how can I throw it away? It's new!".

"Well then, patch it up, add an extra piece", concluded the Saint[38].

If every moment was the right one for the Saint to remind people to be modest in their way of dressing, the best time was in the confessional. It was useless to try and escape his watchful eye.

Two girls from San Marco in Lamis, who attended the nursing school of the Home for the Relief of Suffering, soon found that out. They had booked to confess, but as they usually wore mini-skirts, they realised they couldn't present themselves for confession to Padre Pio dressed in that way. They decided to try and find a solution. Before going to the Friary, they went to

---

[38] Lucietta Pennelli, San Giovanni Rotondo, 5.12.1995.

the boarding school to borrow some longer clothes from their friends. Looking at themselves in these different clothes they said to each other "We just look like clowns".

Dressed in this way they went to church, joined the queue and waited to be called.

Soon afterwards Padre Pio arrived: he stopped to look at the girls and to the confrère who was controlling the queue said: "I am not going to confess those two clowns"[39].

More than once Padre Pio called those people, who changed their normal style of dress to a more modest one, just in order to be near him, clowns.

In the spring of 1967, two mothers who were on their way to confess to Padre Pio with their two daughters, met on the train from Naples to Foggia, and the two girls soon made friends.

Maria Teresa Nicosia a Sicilian from Vittoria (RG) who had already been to see Padre Pio on seeing her new friend's miniskirt advised her to change clothes as soon as she got to San Giovanni Rotondo, because dressed like that that Saint would have surely sent her away.

The two girls went into a shop and the Neapolitan advised by her friend bought a longer skirt that came below the knees and a pair of thick socks. On looking at herself in the mirror the girl said "If my boyfriend could see me he'd think I was a clown!".

The day of the confession with the Padre arrived, and the girl from Naples waited near the confessional; but when her turn came as the grate opened she heard "Go away! I don't confess clowns".

---

[39] This testimony comes from Sister Assunta Baldori, who was the headmistress of the hospital boarding school; Cassano Murge 30.6.1993.

You couldn't fool Padre Pio[40].

We must note however that the Padre in some circumstances was able change his strict line of behaviour, if he thought he could obtain immediate spiritual good for a soul.

Once he acted in a most unexpected way and was tolerant with a woman, who, whilst spending her holidays on the Gargano coast, went to San Giovanni Rotondo as she urgently wished to speak to him.

"Once in church", says Lucietta Pennelli, "The woman stood in front of the Padre's confessional. The Padre finishing a Confession called me and said: "Tell that woman near the holy water fount to go and change otherwise, I won't confess her dressed as she is". She was wearing a short skirt and her arms and legs were bare.

I went to her and told her what the Padre had said. She started to panic and asked me to help her, begging me to give her something to cover her up because she urgently needed to speak to the Padre. I gave her a veil and my coat; but as for stockings I didn't know what to do.

I went to the caretaker's lodge to speak to bro. Gerardo, but the poor friar said it was impossible for him to help us. Then a little embarrassed he said "I have got a long pair of woollen socks that I use to go to town when it's snowing".

I took them and God knows how the woman managed to put them on. Then with her shoes in her hands because she couldn't get them on she went to the confessional. After a brief wait she managed to speak to Padre Pio who, at the end of her confession, gave her absolution, comforted her and sent her home perfectly serene".

---

[40] Concetta Tomasi in Nicosia, Vittoria 3.6.1998.

The recall to decency had been strictly made, but the Padre had given priority to something else. If the Spirit led him to soul to help or save, fixed schemes no longer existed for the holy confessor[41].

Another thing to point out. The Padre wanted women to be discreet also in their use of make-up.

One day going back to his room after giving out communion, he found that the thumb and finger of his right hand were marked with lipstick. Showing his fingers to his confrères he complained about the excessive use of make-up by women, saying: "Giving out communion you dirty your fingers and then you dirty the lips of those who come next".

Fr. Marcello Lepore intervened saying: "But Father all women use lipstick today".

And Padre Pio: "That's the justification: everybody does it. You by reasoning in this way are ruining the Church".

"But what should we do, send them away?", asked the brother.

"Yes, sometimes" replied the Padre.

"No, we can't do that, If you send them away, they'll come back but if we do, they won't".

Padre Pio: "Better to have a few convinced faithful than a lot of people without faith"[42].

4. Shame of showing one's faith

One of the duty of a good Christian is to show others his own faith especially through a worthy way of living. This rep-

---

[41]   Lucietta Pennelli, San Giovanni Rotondo 4.12.95.

[42]   Fr. Marcello Lepore, Foggia 11.3.1997.

resents a witness of the goodness of their faith and an implicit invitation to those around them to come closer to this faith. In this way every believer becomes a missionary who spreads God's word, not with sermons and lectures but by example. The saints are Christ's best witnesses.

Jesus tells us that holy living gives glory to God. The Master says: *"Your light must shine so brightly before men that they can see your good works and glorify your Father who is in Heaven"* (Mt.5,16.).

However Christ's followers must not think they are exempt from spreading their creed and cultivate a missionary conscience within themselves. Evangelisation is not only trusted to the Pope and Bishops. John Paul in the Redemptoris missio reminds us that this "mission is for all Christians, all dioceses, parishes, institutions and ecclesiastical associations" (n. 2).

There are certain circumstances in which the defence of one's faith is obligatory. Not only when God is insulted, but also when the Church institutions are contested: the Christian cannot hide away, he must come forth. St. Paul calls the attention of his Disciple Timothy to this truth: *"Do not blush then, for the witness thou bearest to Our Lord"* (2Tm 1,8).

Let's see what Padre Pio teaches about this.

A young man went to confess to him and the first thing he said was: "In my part of the country, Emilia Romagna, people swear a lot and I out of respect don't always say something to those blasphemers".

The Saint said: "Remember that Jesus said: *"Who is ashamed of acknowledging me before men, I too will be ashamed of acknowledging him before my Father"* (Mark 8,38) and he sent the young man away.

The poor penitent was quite upset but quickly went to another priest who calmed him down assuring him that the Padre would certainly remember him in his prayers.

So it was as we are assured by he who gave us this testimony.

"Even if I never returned again to San Giovanni Rotondo the tie with Padre Pio was never broken; my mother in fact when she needed some advice wrote to Federico Abresh, the Saint's first photographer so that he would ask the Padre to give some light to a problem and a prompt reply always arrived. Finally, a priest that I thought of as my confessor was going to San Giovanni Rotondo and I asked him to ask Padre Pio if he would accept me as a spiritual son. My joy was great when at the priest's return he told me that the Padre had included me amongst the people who formed his great family; so what the priest, who comforted me after Padre Pio had sent me away, assured me did come true"[43].

Other than honouring the name of God, Padre Pio heartily felt that the Church and the Pope should be respected.

Fr. Emanuele Grassi da Riccia, Capuchin friar, speaking to the niece of a Cardinal, noticed that she had a strong aversion towards his beloved brother Padre Pio; naturally enough this upset and displeased him. After many arguments he finally convinced her to go down to San Giovanni Rotondo to personally see for herself what kind of person the Padre was without judging him on hearsay.

The meeting was very upsetting for her. The Saint as soon as he saw her said: "Shame on you, you weren't able to defend your religion". In fact during her train journey she was with people who not only spoke badly of the Church but cursed it. She hadn't said a word for the whole journey.

---

[43]   Libero F., Genova, 20.4.1995.

She accepted the reproof and was convinced that the Padre was not only a man of God but that he was illuminated by Him and could read one's conscience and give soul's the guide for their spiritual well-being[44].

As for the Pope, Padre Pio didn't allow any disrespect.

Mirenda Francesco di Nicastro tells us of a meeting that was dramatic and at the same time mysterious with the Saint. "I confessed to Padre Pio and amongst other things I expressed my perplexity saying: "Father I was surprised and troubled that Pope John XXIII received in the Vatican and spoke to Agiubey, the son-in-law of Kruschev (the head of the communist party)".

As soon as Padre Pio heard this he shouted: "How dare you offend Our Holy Father! We owe the Holy Father obedience and respect. Get out!".

I, shocked at this reaction said: "Father please absolve me. How can I return here again? I live in Sicily and due to my job I will be unable to come back!".

Padre Pio tapping the kneeling stool with his fingertips said: "You will never come back here again".

"But at least bless me", I begged. He blessed me and I moved away from the confessional.

When I went out, I told my wife the Padre's last words and we made the mostgloomy suppositions about my probable end. I really felt terrible. I also spoke to the Father Guardian of the convent Fr. Carmelo di Donato from San Giovanni in Galdo, who reassured me, telling me that I had misinterpreted the Father's words. He advised me to book a new Confession with

---

[44] Fr. Emanuele Grassi da Riccia, capuchin, San Giovanni Rotondo 13,11,1996.

Padre Pio and ask someone who lived in the town to telegram me when my turn was almost due.

That's what I did; together with a friend I went to the booking office, signed and left. The telegram however never arrived. I was on pins as the days passed with no news. My wife seeing my agitation advised me to leave for San Giovanni Rotondo without waiting any longer.

I left with my son in a Fiat "five-hundred". As soon as I arrived on the Gargano I went to the booking office, but Fr. Adriano Leggieri, who let me see the register, showed me that my name, my signature did not appear on the waiting list of those wishing to see Padre Pio. I checked and saw that the friar was right. I was surprised and I wondered what sense all this mystery could have. Still I said to myself: at least I'll be able to say hello to the Padre.

I went to the St. Francis hall, where the Saint was to pass by. As soon as he appeared we all knelt down making way as he walked by. When Padre Pio arrived where I was, he turned to me and smiling said "Ah .you've come back have you?!".

This phrase pleasantly surprised me: the Padre wished to reassure me about my worries of my imminent end. But reflecting on his expression "you will never return again here" I understood that he meant I would never again have knelt at his confessional for Confession".

That was the last time I saw Padre Pio, but the lesson about the respect due to the figure of the Pope has always remained with me[45].

---

[45]   Mirenda Francesco, San Giovanni Rotondo 6.5.1995.

5. Lack of control over the use of one's tongue

Padre Pio was very careful to warn his spiritual children about the sins that could be committed by the tongue. He habitually repeated: "The tongue is a fire that burns a forest". He reminded his spiritual children what the Gospel says: "Men will be brought to account for every thoughtless word they have spoken", that is full of evil (Mt 12.36).

Lies

The Catechism says: "The eight commandment forbids misrepresenting the truth in our relations with others" (n. 2464).

The Holy Confessor could not tolerate this sin even in a venial form.

Nina Campanella had told her family some little lies and she confessed this justifying herself by saying they "didn't harm any body". The Padre replied: "Don't you think about the harm you have done to your own soul?".

Many times people don't realise how much harm they do to their own spiritual structure by not being truthful to others. This behaviour is an implicit refusal to build day by day a basic moral uprightness and undertake to follow it always.

A person who had taken the path of faith and intended to live for God, confessed to having told some little lies, Padre Pio said: "God is truth".

Lucietta Pennelli tells us: "I'm not naturally a liar but once, to avoid trouble, I told my mother a lie. Naturally I had to confess it a day or two later to Padre Pio".

The Padre, as soon as he heard my sins, said: "Nenné (little one), what's your name?".

I replied: "What do you mean Father? It's me".

And Padre Pio: "I asked what's your name?".

"But Father, it's me Lucietta".

The Saint said: "I know that you are Lucietta". And after a brief pause he continued "Lucia…and do you know what Lucia means? It means light and light cannot stay with darkness. Do you understand?"[46].

Sometimes to those who regularly went to Church and often took the Eucharist bread he said: "Do you tell lies with that tongue that receives Jesus?".

A misunderstanding that can occur when the truth is altered is to think that good can come from a lie. Wanda Sellach tells us: "It was during the second World War. I went to Confession and said I had told a lie for a good cause".

And the Padre: "You did ill for a good cause? Just think if I with a lie could stop this war, I still wouldn't tell one. Think how much good I would do!"[47].

The Friary Chronicle illustrates the consistence of the Padre's view-point in this respect.

"Yesterday a gentleman from Florence after confessing to Padre Pio told Fr. Agostino da Campolieto, part of the brotherhood, that he had confessed telling lies. "Father but I told these lies for you. When someone doesn't want to believe what happens here, I brighten things up a bit to encourage them to believe. Is this a sin?".

Padre Pio answered: "Look here my son, if you have a glass of crystal clear fresh water in front of you and you add a droop of wine, you waste that water. If it's fresh and crystal clear you drink it as it is"[48].

---

[46] Lucietta Pennelli, San Giovanni Rotondo 5.12.1995.

[47] Wanda Sellaci, San Giovanni Rotondo, 29.11.1995.

[48] *Chronicle…*, p. 499.

Politics and lies

Fr. Atanasio Lonardo da Teano, a Capuchin friar who for many years was close to Padre Pio left this testimony of the obedience that Enrico Medi gave to his spiritual father.

"Let us make it clear that this great scientist numbered the days he spent close to Padre Pio amongst the best of his life. Especially when he was able to serve at Holy Mass. It was edifying to see him, kneeling down with his hands together like a young altar boy waiting to serve.

Of course he always was present during the half an hour conversation the Padre had with only a few some other close friends on the terrace or in the garden in the late afternoon. I remember an episode in which the professor was the chief player.

One day the discussion was about venial sin, to be exact lies. Padre Pio sustained that lies are always sinful and so it is never right tell them even white lies. Medi who at that time was also a member of Parliament, elected with a great following which could have led to a long prosperous political career, ingenuously turned to Padre Pio and asked him: "Padre aren't we Members of Parliament allowed to tell lies?".

The Padre, who didn't exclude anyone from criticism especially those who had chosen to become his spiritual children and follow him along the Gospel path, quickly replied: "Can it really be you asking me that?". There was a moment of complete silence, whilst all eyes were on the professor whose face had become sad and mortified at the reprimand affectionately given by the Padre.

"Well Father, there is nothing left for me to do but give up my career in politics !" said Enrico.

"What are you waiting for then?" replied the Padre.

Medi, without any hesitation, a few days later handed in his resignation from Parliament . He only reappeared on the political scene, when he was begged by the highest authorities and maybe by Padre Pio himself, to return to politics because the D.C. needed a name that was as prestigious and clean as his[49].

Lies said in Jest

One day Probo Vaccarini said to Padre Pio: "Father, I tell a few lies when I'm in company just to keep everybody happy".

The Padre readily replied: "Eh, do you want to go to Hell jokingly!?".

We have a note from Dr. Piero Melillo with regards to lies said in jest. "One evening, during recreation, I told the Padre something that had happened to me; I exaggerated everything a little to make the tale more enjoyable. As the Padre was not in favour of this exaggeration that was almost a lie, I confessed that I had surely said some amusing lie that certainly was not harmful".

Padre Pio became serious and turning to me said: "A man went into a bar to have a drink and left his bike outside the door. A friend of his who had been following him also entered the bar and for a joke said he had seen someone riding away on the man's bike. At this news the friend "shot out" a terrible swear word". Concluding this tale the Saint asked me: "Who is responsible for this sin? The one who swore or the one who had told a lie in jest?"[50].

---

[49] Testimony written by Fr. Atanasio Lo nardo da Teano, capuchin.
[50] Testimony written by Piero Melillo.

Anger and scorn

The Apostle Paul admonished his Christians of Efeso *"There must be no trace of bitterness, spite or anger amongst you"* (Ef 4, 31).

A spiritual son tells us: "Once whilst in Confession as I was saying my sins the Padre stopped me and asked: "Do you watch what you say when you are speaking?". He had realised I was hot-tempered and impatient. He let me realise that sometimes with hasty words you can lose a friendship.

He then insisted on charity which demands respect for our neighbours"[51].

Padre Pio dedicated particular attention to correct the vice of anger, which often makes people lose control of themselves and do and say senseless things. Therefore in Confession it was almost customary that he asked the penitent: "Did you lose your temper?".

One day the housekeeper of the Sala family had prepared supper and called the children to eat: but it had been like talking to the wind. She lost her temper and shouted: "Damn you, not one of you is moving!".

The day after she went to confess to Padre Pio and as he usually did with her, he led the examination of her conscience, calling her attention to various sins. Then he asked: "Is there anything else?".

She remained silent and the Padre: "Anything else? Speak!".

The poor woman realised the Saint knew what was heavy on her conscience end answered: "I swore at the children because they didn't want to come and eat".

"You wretch", shouted the Padre. "You cursed! Get out!".

---

[51] Quirino Cresti, Chiavari 28.9.1995.

She went away crying.

The following night she dreamt that her mother had come from Sardinia to San Giovanni Rotondo and as there was nothing in the house to make a meal with, Mrs Sala, the children's mother said "Cut a slice of one of the children's bottoms".

The housekeeper replied "No, never!".

So the mother grabbed the smallest child and with a knife cut of a slice of the child's bottom and gave it to her.

The girl was so horrified she screamed out loud and woke up.

"I thought", confided the one giving this testimony "that the dream was a message from the Padre to let me understand what it is to curse your neighbour"[52].

It is upsetting for a Christian that many times he loses his peace of mind for nothing. Giovanna Russo tells us: "One day my sisters had an argument that was caused by a quarrel amongst their children who often fell out with each other. I too was caught up in the quarrel. A few hours later peace returned".

The day after I went to confess to the Padre and when I had finished he asked me: "Is there any more or do you want me to say it?".

Seeing I was embarrassed and dumbstruck he added: "Getting angry in that way! Aren't you ashamed of yourself? At least it could have been for something important".

He gave me penance and absolution. I was so ashamed I didn't go to the part of the confessional to kiss his hand as all the penitents did. I was walking away but he leaned out and called me: he with a smile on his lips traced a large sign of the cross on me-as if to say his reproach was a sign of love. Peace returned to my heart once more"[53].

---

[52] Mariangela Casu, Oristano 21.4.1999.
[53] Giovanna Russo, San Giovanni Rotondo 2.12.1985.

Rumours

As well as the vices of anger St Paul warns the Christians of Ephesians to avoid *"insulting talk or spite of any kind"*(Ef 4.31).

One of the sins for which Padre Pio refused absolution was that of spreading rumours and speaking badly of others, which even those who profess to be…practising Christians often do.

The Catechism teaches that he "who without objectively valid reasons discloses another's faults and failings to .persons who do not know them sins" (n. 2477). The wickedness of the sin is this they destroy the reputation and honour of one's neighbour. Everyone enjoys a natural right to honour his name and reputation without which life becomes difficult or impossible (n. 2479).

Rightly enough the Padre was very severe with those who perhaps unwittingly offended justice and charity.

He said to a penitent: "When you spread rumours about someone it means that you don't love them, you have removed them from your heart. But you must realise that when you take someone from your heart, Jesus also leaves with that brother or sister".

Once when he had been invited to bless a house, when he arrived at the kitchen door he said: "There are snakes here I'm not going in". And to a priest who often went there he told him not to go any more because the people there spread rumours[54].

By spreading rumours one not only lacks charity but makes judgement, going against what Jesus says: *"Judge nobody…"* (Lk 6,37).

---

[54] *Notes…,* September 1993.

With regards to rash judgements, Pietro Cugino remembers: "Padre Pio was very severe when someone admitted this sin: The Padre admonished: "Only God can judge, not we"[55].

To be able to stay within the precepts of the Lord who will himself severely judge those who rise to judge their brothers and sisters, *"As you have judge so will you be judged"* (Mt 7,2), Padre Pio suggested a trick: to avoid giving judgement, one should not make it, otherwise sooner or later all that one has inside ones soul comes out.

"Even if we see a delinquent we cannot judge him: only God can see inside a person's heart; neither can we be scandalised by the mistakes of others, otherwise the Lord allows us to come to blows with the same mistake. If unfortunately we are forced to give judgement, let us do so charitably"[56].

Whenever a penitent in confession admitted to having inadvertently made a mistake in expressing an opinion or having exaggerated a little, the Saint asked: "Have you taken back what you said?"[57].

The Padre also warned his spiritual children about irony. He said one day to Luciano Bellodi from Modena: "To be ironic or humorous you need a heart and a brain and you need to be able to understand who is listening to you, that is the person before you: because irony could deeply hurt someone and go beyond your original intention"[58].

---

[55] Pietro Cugino, San Giovanni Rotondo 7.9.2000.

[56] *Notes…*, 21.2.1985.

[57] *Ibid.*

[58] Testimony written by Liliana Bonichini widow Bellodi, Modena 16.12.1998.

Sister to irony is the cutting quip: to avoid making a mistake first of all you must control your innermost thoughts. It was that which the Saint seemed to want to teach a visitor.

A woman, knowing that a friend of hers was going down to San Giovanni Rotondo, asked her to deliver a letter to Padre Pio with an offering for Holy Mass. The woman put 10,000 lire in an envelope in front of her friend.

It was in the fifties and the go-between seeing the generous offering said to herself: "How much money for a Mass!" When she arrived at San Giovanni Rotondo as soon as she was able she handed him the letter.

The Saint looking at the closed envelope, said a little amused: "How much money for a Mass!". The woman realised who she had before her and accepted the lesson she had been taught"[59].

6. Refusing to forgive others

Forgiveness is the best gift we can give or receive .The etymology of the word in its prefix expresses it perfectly (perdono) per- as in perfection.

We can always expect a gift for our good behaviour. Forgiveness is different: it is destined to those who have done ill and have offended. Forgiveness is given to the defeated and the winners. To those who have lost dignity by doing wicked things.

To give forgiveness is a characteristic of God. Jesus tells us this in the parable of the Prodigal son, as we call it, but we should rename it with the title *"the Father's mercy"*: Forgive-

---

[59]   Wanda Sellaci, San Giovanni Rotondo, 19.12.1996.

ness is given by good souls, the saints, those who try to be like God.

St. Paul urges Christians to forgive, but he makes them understand this is not to be improvised; it must be accompanied with a host of virtues. He writes to the Colossians: *"You are God's chosen people, holy and well-beloved: the livery you wear must be compassion, kindness, humility, gentleness and patience; you must bear with one another's faults, be generous to each other, where someone has given you grounds for complaint. As the Lord has forgiven you, do likewise" (Col 3.12.13).*

The Gospel tells us clearly that forgiveness is for us sinners a need. There are no excuses for those who do not wish to make a gesture in which, overcoming the feeling of rancour you make allowances and excuses for those who have damaged or offended you. They will be excluded from God's forgiveness on Judgement Day. The parable of the ruthless servant, who having had an almost immeasurable debt remitted, ten thousand talents, makes one of his fellow servants be put in prison for not having paid a hundred denarius a ridiculous sum in comparison with the remittance received: 600,000 times inferior, is terrifying. However the ruthless man is condemned by the king who "gives him to the tormentors till he should to pay all that was due to him".

Jesus concludes *"So likewise shall my heavenly Father do also unto if ye, from your hearts forgive not every one of his brothers their trespasses"* (Mt 18-23-25).

Francis of Assisi weaving his praises to God through the beauty of creation sings: *"Blessed be they who forgive for love of you"*[60].

---

[60] FONTI FRANCESCANE, *Il Cantico delle Creature*, Ed. Movimento francescano, Assisi 1977, 178, n.263.

The life of Padre Pio was scattered with misunderstandings and mortifications of which he never showed the slightest resentment. He always forgave and he wished his children would follow his example.

To Sister Pura Pagani who in Confession said she had been wronged and upset in the ecclesiastic environment the Padre said: *"You must forgive I too have forgiven"*[61].

There is a rather mysterious episode narrated by Mario Sanci about forgiveness. "In my employment office during a heated discussion a worker gave me a strong blow. He was reported to the police and they went to look for him to arrest him. He was too afraid to even go home to sleep. It was in the Easter period 1956.

After a lot of persuasion by my friends I dropped the charge.

A long time afterwards I went to San Giovanni Rotondo to confess to Padre Pio. As soon as I knelt down the Padre asked: "Have you been charitable to some father, head of a family?".

My thought immediately flew to the dropped charge and I answered: "Yes Father, but it cost me a slap". As soon as I said this I saw the Padre bend to one side and put his hand on his cheek as if he was receiving that same slap at that moment. I felt embarrassed and saddened.

The Saint got up and began: "How long is it since your last confession". I confessed and he gave me absolution .

Every now and then I think about this episode. I think that the Padre wanted to show me that in truth I really had given him a slap because, even though I was claiming to be his spiritual son, I hadn't wanted to forgive the person who had offended me: but I must add that since that day, when I am before

---

[61] Sr. Pura Pagani, Mozzecane (VE) 10.5.1995.

the crucifix I see how many blows and whiplashes I have given Jesus through my sins. That lesson was for my well-being"[62]. Mario Sanci, Salemi (TR) 4.11.1996.

Padre Pio habitually told penitents and his Spiritual children to think of and remember Jesus nailed to the cross for our faults when they found it difficult to forgive someone.

A woman confessed to Padre Pio and when she had finished confessing she waited for the Padre to speak; he asked her: "Anything else?".

When she replied no the confessor repeated the question At the second no the Saint asked: "How are things between you and your brother? How are you getting on?".

"He doesn't speak to me but it's not my fault. He's been bad to me and drifted away from me. I don't know what to do", answered the penitent.

"Go and make peace" said the Saint.

"But Father he's the one who behaved badly to me not vice-versa", the penitent said to justify herself.

To which the Saint said "And Jesus what had he done wrong when he was put on the cross. Didn't he die for the faults of others and for yours?". The Padre refused to give her absolution[63].

We must note that the Padre had truly been offended and upset in his dignity and honour and knew exactly how it felt. How many affronts and insults he suffered on his own back.

A young married woman who told Padre Pio she was continually humiliated by her husband's family, heard the Holy Confessor tell her with a voice full of gentleness and under-

---

[62]   Mario Sanci, Salemi (TR) 4.11.1996.

[63]   Testimony from Daniele Natale recorded by Franco Dal Lago Thiene 10.5.1997.

standing: "You have a heart full of hate for your husband's relatives. You have reason to be so angry because you are in the right, but for the love of God you must forgive"[64].

The Padre showed the penitent the way to inner peace. The reason why we harden our hearts against those who have offended us is that we defend ourselves by wishing to give back what we received. The ancient law of *an eye for an eye, a tooth for a tooth,* if on one hand we exclude charity towards each other, on the other hand we take away our own love of life. The Saint also teaches that the motivation of forgiveness is all and only in the love we give to God, to whom in truth we make a humble gift of our suffering, without asking for revenge.

Even for S.L., a teacher who had also suffered a great injustice which had marked her whole life, there was understanding and a welcome from the Padre but in a very particular way.

In 1956 she went to San Giovanni Rotondo but she was a little sceptical towards Padre Pio. When she saw that women let him touch their rosary beads after Confession she said "It's fetishism", but soon after she added, like a prayer: "Lord if this friar is really a saint give me a sign".

That night at 2-30 am she awoke smelling an intense perfume of roses. She wondered where it could come from: she had no bottles of perfume with her and on her bedside table there was only the cigarette end she had put out before falling asleep.

In the morning she wanted to check if there was a rose garden near the boarding house where she was staying; but there was nothing! Going to church she confessed to Padre Pio the sin which lay heaviest on her conscience: "I curse my ex-fiancée's mother because she was the cause of our break-up and

---

[64]   Ippolita Ricciardi, Foggia 22.12.1998

possible marriage".

Padre Pio shouted at her "and who are you to judge others? When you are repentant come back here" and he slammed the grate of the confessional in her face.

Once back in her hotel in the grips of a hysterical crisis she began to rail "What kind of saint is this, who hasn't given me a word of comfort to me who has been wronged!? I expected compassion and found judgement!", she continued in this way but her anger grew as the time passed.

Suddenly she smelt the perfume of violets. She was silenced. Then she asked her friends it they too could smell it. They answered no. She realised then that Padre Pio was close to her despite his harsh words.

Within a month she had calmed down. But with the passing of time she realised to astonishment that in her heart there was no longer a trace of hate. After a month she returned to San Giovanni Rotondo and the Padre gave her absolution[65].

The Saint also taught in Confession the method to be in the right mood to forgive: to create an interior predisposition for forgiveness, in a way that any offence would not find one unprepared but ready to be clement.

He asked a penitent one day: "do you know how to examine your conscience?".

The penitent was not ready to give an answer and the Padre continued "Let's see, if someone does something against you how do you behave?".

The penitent replied: "Well then Father, first I react then I

---

[65] The witness prefers to remain anonymous. The testimony was given in Campobasso on 5.9.2002.

repent and try hard to forgive".

"You make a mistake my son. If someone does something wrong, you have to already forgive him whilst he is doing it without reacting. Forgiveness after reacting is rather late"[66].

That the Padre had a predisposition for forgiveness is shown by a testimony. Cleonice Morcaldi remembers that in the twenties, during the period in a which certain people from the town let slanderous voices against Padre Pio arrive to Rome, a professional man from San Giovanni Rotondo, returning from the capital where he had gone to speak against the Saint, called in the Friary.

A friar who was busy doing things wanted to stop the man from going to the sacristy where the Padre was confessing. The Saint told the brother to let the doctor pass. When this fellow was near him, calling him by name he exclaimed: "Eh, how long have you been away! Give me a hug!".

And he hugged him in front of everybody[67].

The Padre included antipathy and uncalled for instinctive aversion in the sphere of hate. In confession a woman said: "Father I find it hard to greet people I don't like", and Padre Pio promptly replied: "So do pagans"[68].

7. Theft

Stealing is a sin against the seventh commandment (cf. Es.20, 15; Dt 5,19). As the catechism recites, the Divine Law "forbids unjustly taking or keeping the goods of one's neighbour and wronging him in any way with respect to his goods".

---

[66] Testimony written by Wanda Sellach.
[67] *Ibid.*
[68] Elena Santuliana, Riva del Garda 23.3.1996.

Jesus reminds us of this *"Do not steal"* (Mt 19.18).

If in everyone there is an instinctive refusal to subtract wealth, such as money or goods, from others by directly taking things, often carrying out an activity an which wealth is involved one , can be tempted to take what belongs to others by trickery: fraud. The evangelist Mark amongst the precepts of the Decalogue proposed by Jesus see Matthew quoted above and Luke 18,20, has also "Do not cheat" (cf. Mk10,19).

Fraud is a camouflaged theft which Padre Pio unmasked. Often the penitent heard themselves called "thief" A business man, a house agent and others have confessed this to us.

1.To a penitent, who falsified to his advantage goods delivery receipts, the Saint didn't even give the time to kneel down and shouted at him, "Get out you thief...! Go and repair the damage that you have done to your town".

The man returned to his town and put things straight, risking being reported to the Police and losing his job. After two or three months he returned to San Giovanni Rotondo to confess. When he was at Padre Pio's feet he quickly confessed he had stolen, expecting that the Padre would add more to what he had said before, but the Holy Confessor just asked him to continue his confession and at the end gave him absolution.

The penitent was amazed by Padre Pio's indulgence and almost not believing asked "Father, do you recognise me?".

"A face like yours, once seen is not forgotten" said God's servant. In the answer as well as the assurance to go in peace because he had really been forgiven there was still a warning[69].

2. A young timber merchant was on quite good terms with

---

[69] This testimony anonymous for obvious reasons was given on 9.10.1999.

Fr. Nazareno Caselli, Capuchin friar, and one day he informed him that he was going to San Giovanni Rotondo to confess to Padre Pio. The wise and witty friar looked him in the eye and said: "Do your washing well because Padre Pio has good eyes".

When the young man arrived on the Gargano he booked a Confession. On the day his turn arrived as soon as he knelt down, the Padre shouted "First of all go and sort out that wood consignment!".

He returned to Emilia disappointed and furious and decided he would never go again to see the friar of whom everyone spoke well and considered a saint. However the cry of the Padre touched his conscience and like a wood-worm ate into his brain. He thought again about his insane proposal and decided against it; he sorted things out with regards to "that consignment" in which he had cheated about the weight and returned to San Giovanni Rotondo.

He confessed. Padre Pio listened like a father, gave him absolution and peace once more[70].

8. Magic

A phenomenon which saddens many true believers today is that many people even though they say they are Christians turn to magicians for various advice and answers or to find solutions to problems of various types.

Padre Pio it goes without saying forbade any form or use of the occult or spiritualism. A Venetian lady tells us: "I confessed to Padre Pio on November 3rd 1948. Amongst other things I

---

[70] Fr. Nazareno Caselli, Sassuolo (MO) 14.9.2003.

said our family was worried because an aunt read cards.

The Padre in a stern tone said: "Throw those things away as soon as possible"[71].

The testimony which follows, by Anna Di Leonardo, gives us more details about why she turned to a magician.

But the Padre's answer was just as hard.

One day she went to his confessional and confessed she had been to a fortune teller.

The Saint asked: "Why on earth did you go?".

"Father I was a bit down and disheartened because everything was going wrong and I hoped for some good news".

The Padre said: "Don't go there again because if you go and then come back to me, the blows will all be for you"[72].

Why did the Padre threaten to make an example of this poor girl, who at her wits end, had turned to fortune tellers.

Amongst the reasons why people turn to fortune tellers are "The research for consolation and reassurance" which is the case of the woman quoted above, the need for total explanations, a search for salvation from pain the risk of existence and the uncertainties of the future" which one wishes to see unveiled[73].

We must admit that man, once he declares his impotence, can turn to God's world or that of Satan. From the latter who works through his accomplices who have sold themselves to him for vile interests, you can expect nothing of any good.

---

[71]   Rita Rizzetti, Thiene, 25.5.1996

[72]   Anna Di Leonardo, San Giovanni Rotondo 14.5.1999.

[73]   From *I soldi del diavolo,* edited by ISPES, via Terme Traiano 5, Roma 1989, quoted by RAUL SALVUCCI in *Indicazioni pastorali di un esorcista,* Editrice Ancora Milano, 1994, 21.

Satan is the essence of Evil .Good can never come from evil. Jesus says *"Do men gather grapes of thorns or figs of this-tles?"* (Mt 7.16).

Padre Pio wished that the demon was not even mentioned by his spiritual children. He in fact, writing to spiritual fathers about hidden dangers held by the spirit of evil never used his specific name. Quoting from the first volume of the epistolary of the Saint the authors of that edition wrote: "Purely for cu-riosity we give the long list of expressions used by Padre Pio to describe with witty irony and a pinch of humour his rival. Here is what is found in his epistolary correspondence from January 1911 to September 1915: *big whiskers, whiskers, the ogre, scoundrel, miserable evil spirit, wretch, filthy wretch, foul Beast, woeful wretch, hideous faces, impure spirit, those scoundrels, wicked spirit, horrible beast, ,accursed beast, in-famous apostate, impure apostates, gallows-bird, howling wild beasts, malignant deceiver, prince of darkness*[74].

Only reading these things makes one shiver and to think that some people believe they can gain benefit by putting their hand into this bag of poisonous snakes!

Others claim to find benefit for their faith by practising white magic. Padre Pio saw this as a mistaken way to approach God's world.

Luciano Livellara from Milan tells us: "I attended so called white magic spiritual séances, where they called up spirits of the past to whom they asked questions about the hereafter. During Confession I spoke about this to the Padre who told me "I don't say that the things that take place are all foolishness

---

[74]   *Letters* I, 129.

or that they are true. No, however don't go to those reunions any more".

I quickly replied "Father I must confess that since I have attended these séances I believe more in the supernatural".

And Padre Pio: "This is not the way that Jesus taught. Don't go again: the devil could play an evil trick on you"[75].

Therefore the so called white magic too can be a means and a way in which the evil spirit can work.

A testimony offered to us by bro. Daniele Natale, confirms the Padre's thought on the subject and seems to continue the speech which is quoted above.

Our brother tells us: "In 1955 I received a letter from Giselda De Cecco from Fara S.Martino. I'll read it to you: "I have met a person who speaks to the Holy Souls in Purgatory. She tells me lots of good things, she has encouraged me to pray and do lots of acts of charity. I wish to know what Padre Pio's opinion is. Should I continue to go or not? What ever he tells me I will do".

One day I went out into the garden with the Padre and we sat on a little wall near the bowling field. I read him the letter and added: "Father what shall I answer?".

"My son", said the Saint, "we have God's commandments, we have the Gospel and the sacramental Jesus in our midst".

"Yes Father, but this woman wants a definite answer ,a yes or no; should she go to the meetings or not".

"I will repeat, we have the commandments, we have the Gospel we have Jesus in our midst", answered Padre Pio.

"Father I understand but I want a yes or no to send her".

And the Saint with patience: "Let's admit that nine times

75   Luciano Livellara, Chiavari 4.12.1994.

it is the voice of goodness which speaks. And if just once the enemy turns into a devil and damages a soul? Try and sort that out afterwards!"[76].

This is how Padre Pio brings Jesus and his word to the centre of our search for truth, putting us on our guard from the "Enemy" which can assert itself in our thirst for assurances.

The reason why people do not have faith in Jesus as the saviour of all men, and instead attempt dangerous adventures of which sometimes there is no return is the drifting away from the conception and practice of religion in life. So man left alone, at his own mercy, goes to look for truth health and joy where there is sure death.

Justly the Church to avoid this race to spiritual suicide, in its teachings reminds us: "All forms of divination are to be rejected: recourse to Satan or demons, conjuring up the dead or others practices falsely supposed to "unveil" the future.

All practises of magic or sorcery by which one attempts to tame occult powers, so as to place them at one's service and a have a supernatural power over others, even if this were for the sake of restoring their health, are gravely contrary to the virtue of religion. These practices are even more to be condemned when accompanied by the intention of harming someone, or when they have recourse to the intervention of demons[77].

---

[76] Bro. Daniele Natale, Cerignola 3.10.1986.
[77] Catechismo…, n. 2116, 2117.

9. Two causes of suffering for Padre Pio

Two sins that particularly troubled the Padre in the confessional and without doubt made him severe were those of not attending Mass on Holy days and cursing.

To Fr. Carmelo Durante, who had told him of the grumbling of those who had been sent away from the confessional without a second thought, he said: "But how can you give absolution to those who don't go to Mass on Sundays and those who curse offending God, the Holy Mother and the Saints?"[78].

Curses

The Padre loved God so much he could not accept or tolerate the least lack of respect towards Him.

A family from Milan were going through a very difficult patch. Sickness was commonplace and the mother often complained saying God was very hard on them and not like a father.

I spoke of her painful situation to Padre Pio, to ask for the help of his prayers, but he was clearly displeased by her attitude showing lack of submission to what God can allow for the sanctification of his own children and exclaimed "Ah, yes, now they are in the right!" and added no more.

I remember that once, whilst he was returning to his cell after the women's Confession, a priest said to him: "Padre, why doesn't the Lord give us more grace, so that we are not always so mediocre?".

And the Saint, as if annoyed: "Ah, yes, now it is God's fault

---

[78]   Fr. Carmelo Durante, Larino (CB) Summer 1986.

is it!? Why don't you say that we don't give all our will and all our strength?"[79].

But Padre Pio was really wounded to the heart when he heard that God was insulted by curses, whose evil lies in the words used against him which not only reproach but are full of challenge and hate.

How much the Padre suffered is shown by a testimony given to us by bro. Daniele Natale taken from a man who was converted following a Confession to the Saint.

1. He heard talk of Padre Pio in the family, when an aunt who had been suffering with a tumour, was cured through his prayers.

His mother had sent a telegram to the Saint asking for his help. She had this answer: "I will pray for your sister until the Lord cures her. I will stay with my arms uplifted, so that He will listen to us". This telegram was put under the patients pillow and a little later the sick woman opened her eyes as if she was coming back from another world and said: "A friar came to see me and he said "Arise you are cured." They showed her a photo of Padre Pio and in it she recognised her benefactor. The aunt went back to her normal life, she was so well she managed to look after her vegetable garden.

This fellow was as lorry driver and often passed through Puglia and thought about going to see the friar who obtained graces and miracles for people who were suffering. So one day he decided to go up to San Giovanni Rotondo to confess.

"Padre Pio", he says, was of an extreme patience and delicacy with him.

"How long is it since your last Confession?", asked the Holy Confessor.

---

79 Personal diary.

"It must be five or six years" answered the unprepared penitent, vaguely indicating the time of his last Confession.

"For you five or six are the same aren't they? Don't you know it is a sin to fail to fulfil one's Easter duties?".

The other remained in silence and the Padre went on to the next question.

"Have you been going to Mass on Sundays?".

"No I missed it".

"How many times?".

"Father, I don't know; if you ask me when I did go maybe I'll be able to answer".

"My son, Confession is a serious business and you should prepare well for it".

Pare Pio paused and continued, "But what sins do you remember?".

"I cursed".

The Padre's face saddened and he asked "Who did you curse?".

"Jesus and Our Lady", replied the other.

When he heard that these Holy names had been besmeared Padre Pio, said the penitent, looked as if he had been stabbed in the heart".

"Really, against Jesus and Our Lady?", he murmured quite overcome, as he collapsed against the kneeling stool.

After a brief pause "What more could they do for us than what they have already done?".

At the Padre's question of how many times the man had offended the Lord and his Mother the penitent could not answer.

"But how is it possible you did something so atrocious without even realising it!?", said the Holy Confessor, and after a while "my son get up and go away …come back another time. Do not curse any more".

"Father, but I have come to you because I want to be helped to save my soul", objected the penitent, who had begun to realise the beauty of living in God's Grace.

"That's the reason I am sending you away: I want to help you save your soul." And the Saint ended the conversation.

The penitent concludes speaking to bro. Daniele: "I left the confessional and left for my town, but every time I found myself ready to curse, the image of Padre Pio collapsed as I saw him when I was kneeling in the confessional came into my mind. So I forcibly stopped myself from swearing. I started to follow God's law and attend church.

Many other things changed in my life after my meeting with Padre Pio. From being a workman I became the owner of three marble quarries and numerous means of transport. I also have a beautiful family that is my greatest satisfaction[80].

2. Emilia was a very sweet person who had married a man who was very attractive but not very faithful. She became ill with rheumatic arthritis and because it was so painful she could no longer go with her husband to the various hotels he managed.

One day a young woman arrived on her doorstep: Emilia's husband had got the girl pregnant and she had been thrown out of her home. Emila even though she had been humiliated and betrayed gave the girl hospitality and tried to pacify the girl's family promising to look after the future baby.

A never ending series of other tragic circumstances had so exasperated her to make her habitually curse God.

At the beginning of the nineteen fifties some priests from her town invited her to join them on a trip to San Giovanni

---

[80]   Bro. Daniele Natale, Cerignola 2.10.1986.

Rotondo. She accepted the invitation and once on the Gargano decided to confess to Padre Pio.

Going towards the confessional she hadn't even had time to make the sign of the cross when the Saint in a fatherly but stern voice shouted: "Don't curse again, don't curse again!". The poor woman started to sob and as she was so upset she couldn't say a single word.

Padre Pio spoke to her very gently, telling her all the sins she had prepared to confess. From that day on, Emilia never swore again following the admonishment shouted at her by the Holy Man. In exchange for her promise not to curse, the Saint let her feel his protection.

After the beak up of her marriage, to make a living during the Second World War, she opened a bread shop, but her good heart got her into trouble with the law. In a quick check-up at the end of the month, she realised that the receipts for seven quintals of bread were missing She had given the bread to the poor hungry folk.

On hearing that the yearly control by the police was due she ran to the Capuchin's church which was next to her shop, to pray that this irregularity would not be too harshly punished. A sudden bombing hit the shop destroying the counter where the documents were kept. So she was freed from all her worries[81].

3. It often happened that it was the Holy Confessor himself who through the light of the Holy Spirit saw the mark of this terrible sin within the soul.

Cesare Salvucci came down from the Marche Region with a friend to take some furniture to Monte Sant'Angelo (FG). Whilst the were making the last climb up the road before

---

[81]   Luciana Chini, Moena (TN) 4.9.2003

reaching their destination the lorry broke down and stopped. The driver lost his temper and was very angry.

The day after the two went to San Giovanni Rotondo where a sister of Cesare lived. Through her he arranged a Confession with Padre Pio. First of all the friend went in. The Padre didn't even let him kneel down but sent him away reproaching him severely.

Then it was Cesare's turn who began his confession and said: "I lost my temper".

Padre Pio shouted: "You wretch, you cursed Our Mother! What has Our Lady done to you?". And he sent him away[82].

4. From another testimony we realise another truth that often escapes us, when we speak of cursing: the demon is so close to those who take the name of God in vain as to become like him.

In a hotel in San Giovanni Rotondo, you couldn't rest by day or by night because there was a little girl who shouted and screamed as if she were possessed by the devil. Her cries were frightening. Her mother took her to church every day in the hope that Padre Pio would free her from this evil spirit. Even here the commotion that took place was indescribable.

One morning after the women's Confession whilst crossing the church to go back to the Friary, Padre Pio found himself in front of the energumen who screamed horribly and was held back with difficulty by two or three men the Saint, tired of all this turmoil stamped on her foot and then gave her a violent slap on her head shouting "Now that's enough!".

The little girl fell lifeless to the ground. The Padre told a doctor who was present to take her to St. Michael the nearby

---

[82]   Cesare Salvucci, San Giovanni Rotondo 14.5.1999.

shrine of Monte Sant'Angelo about twenty or so kilometres away.

Luciano Livellara, from Milan took the girl and her mother in his car and in another car there was the doctor and a robust friar whom Padre Pio had told to accompany the pilgrims.

When they arrived at their destination they entered the grotto where St. Michael had appeared. The little girl came to but there was no way to get her to go near the altar dedicated to the Archangel. The chauffeur, the doctor, the friar and another man who had joined them were unable to hold still this tiny being who wriggled away.

There was a lucky break for these willing helpers, the friar with a quick energetic move managed to grip the little girl's hand and touch the altar of St. Michael. The little girl fell to the floor as if she had been struck.

She reawakened a little later, completely relaxed and peaceful as if nothing had happened and sweetly asked: "Mummy will you buy me an ice-cream?".

Once this wish had been satisfied, the little group returned to San Giovanni Rotondo to inform and thank the Padre, who turned to the mother and said: "Tell your husband not to curse anymore or the demons will return"[83].

Neglecting the Eucharist

Many who went to confess to Padre Pio were astonished if not scandalized, when on hearing they had not been to mass on Sunday, he stopped the Confession and sent them away. Often you heard someone complaining. "I've come from far away, I

---

83   Luciano Livellara, Chiavari 6.12.1994.

booked a Confession. I waited spending time and money and Padre Pio is sending me away for a sin like this".

For these people not taking part in Sunday Mass was a "sin like this", as if to say hardly a sin at all.

The Vatican Council II reminds us: "Our Saviour during the last Supper, on the night he was betrayed, established the Eucharistic sacrifice of his Flesh and of his Blood, in order to perpetuate in the centuries to come, until his return, the sacrifice of the cross, and to entrust his beloved bride, the Church with the memorial of his Death and Resurrection" (S.C. n.47).

It should be noted that in the *memorial* the same actions of he who instituted it, are repeated; so if Jesus on the cross offered himself to the Padre in atonement for our sins, we celebrating the Eucharist, obeying his words: "*Do this in memory of me*" (cf. Lk 22-19), from the altar we lift up towards heaven the same victim of Calvary, thinking of him as the saviour of our sins and from divine anger.

Let us remember: Mass "is the making present and sacramental offering of this unique sacrifice" of Christ our Saviour[84].

It is necessary to remember that, if we through his presence, not only spiritual but physical, do not express our wish to be saved, we will be excluded from redemption.

"The Eucharist is the heart and summit of the Church's life, through this sacrifice Christ spreads the grace of the salvation on his Body" mystic body which is us, his Church[85].

However, just speaking of Italy, only 20% of Catholics go to mass. The percentage of those who take communion is much lower, ignoring what Jesus said: "*I myself am the living bread*

---

[84] *Catechismo*, n. 1362.
[85] *Catechismo*, n. 1407.

which came down from heaven: if any man eat of this bread, he shall live for ever". The gentle Master tells us the negative side too. *"You can have no life in yourselves, unless you eat the flesh of the Son of Man"* (John 6,51.53).

St. Theresa of the Child Jesus remarked about those who do not nourish themselves with the bread of heaven: "When the devil manages to keep a soul away from Holy Communion it has achieved its aim"[86].

In the face of the tremendous reality, underlined by the Saint of Lisieux, how could Padre Pio keep calm and not shake with all the prophetic force he possessed those who slept peacefully with regards to a situation of superficiality which could cause the death of their soul?

We must also note another fact: Those who came to ask the Padre for his help, by neglecting the Eucharist didn't realise that the Saint drew all his force of intercession through Jesus in Holy Mass, in which he renewing the passion and death of the Son of God, united his blood with that of the divine victim to atone for the wickedness of all men all over the world, but especially for those who at San Giovanni Rotondo drew around him as their protector.

To report the severity shown by the Holy Confessor to those penitents who neglected the Eucharist could seem superfluous as there is a large amount of literature dedicated to this subject. However a hint will not go amiss in this examination of the sins the Saint considered to be very serious.

1. A doctor from Taranto, at the beginning of the fifties,

---

[86]   SANTA TERESA DI GESU' BAMBINO, *Pensieri*, Ed. OCD, Morena (Roma) 2001, 25.

knelt one day at the Padre's feet to confess. He made his confession and remained in silence.

Padre Pio asked if there was anything else to add: when the answer of no was given the Padre speaking in the dialect of Taranto said: "Remember that on feast days you can't miss even one mass, because it is a mortal sin".

As the young man was careful and punctual in fulfilling his religious duties, he was surprised about what Padre Pio said; but thinking carefully he remembered that in fact, a few months before one Sunday he had missed Mass[87].

2. Most unusual is what happened to Domenico Musto from Naples. He had gone to San Giovanni Rotondo out of curiosity for what was said about Padre Pio.

After spending a few days on the Gargano, one afternoon he joined other men in the sacristy who were waiting to speak to the Holy Friar in confession.

When his turn came he moved the curtain which separated the sacristy from the Confession area, he had just knelt down, when the Padre, with a decisive gesture signalled him to go away.

He, not understanding, remained where he was.

The Padre, who had his eyes closed and was leaning his head on his right hand, with his elbow resting against the higher part of the kneeling stool, finally looked at him and said: "Haven't you understood that you have to go?".

"But I must confess replied the man".

And the Padre a little ironically "oh yes, you have to confess do you?". After staring at him he added "You are a lawyer aren't you?". The penitent affirmed this was so. The Padre

---

[87]   San Giovanni Rotondo, October 1994.

continued: "You are a good lawyer for others but a bad one for yourself, because you don't take care of your spiritual interests. You don't go to Mass!".

The Saint paused and then continued "Start going to Mass and in six months come back, that is, if I am still here". It was the beginning of 1968.

The lawyer, who had calmed down went away.

He returned after the given period and was welcomed by Padre Pio. Today he never misses a Mass and if for some reason, not due to him, he cannot keep his promise to the Padre "he sees, he claims, "the Padre's severe look which reproaches him".

We must add that the Saint entered in the life of this penitent not only as a doctor of his soul, but also of his body. In fact when he was struck by a serious illness Padre Pio saved him from a sure death[88].

10. Some clarifications

The examination of some sins "as seen" by Padre Pio ends here. It does not claim to be complete or conclusive. We wish now to add some notes to highlight ordinary matters.

The root of all evil

It sometimes happens when we run into some sin that we look for a reason to lessen or excuse our fault. We blame circumstances or peoples without clearly admitting our fault.

---

[88] Domenico Musto, Campitello Matese (CB), Winter 1987.

Naturally we don't try.

To excuse the demon that tempts us. This old story was started by our ancestors in their earthly paradise. However according to Padre Pio the real origin of evil is man's egoism.

One day the Padre asked a spiritual daughter: "Do you know what evil is called?".

"It's called Satan", she replied.

"No it isn't", answered the Saint.

"The Devil", added the spiritual daughter.

"No", once more said the Saint.

"Demon?".

"No" asserted for the third time Padre Pio.

"Well, then please tell me what it is called".

Padre Pio: "It is called "I" and we must stab it each time it appears, because it never dies"[89].

St. Thomas Aquinas writes about the origin of moral evil: "Egoism, that is the disorderly love of oneself, is the cause of all sin".

St. Catherine of Siena says "Love of oneself, which removes charity and delight, is the beginning and foundation of all evil".

This explanation of the assertions of the holy doctors of the Church is the following: "Egoism is the denial of moral order, because it establishes one's own self as goodness and pushes the soul despite its limitations and dependence to take the place of the final and infinite goodness which is God"[90].

---

[89]   E. Mori, May 1993.
[90]   See P. A. DAGNINO, *La vita interiore*, Ed. Paoline 1960, 878-879.

Calling sin by its right name

In Confession at the moment when we are about to open our soul to God's minister, we can become so upset and overcome with shame that we do not make a clear accurate Confession.

The Catechism of the Catholic Church reminds us that "those who fail to do so and knowingly withhold some sins, place nothing before the divine goodness for remission through the mediation of the priest; for if the sick person is too ashamed to show the doctor his wound, the medicine cannot heal what it does not know"(1456).

With regards to the lack of clarity in the Confession of sins we have an enjoyable tale to tell which also shows Padre Pio's wit.

Lucia Penelli tells us: "I had promised the Padre I wouldn't have danced again and I kept my promise of not going to family parties where I could have broken my word, however one day it was my cousin's wedding and all my family were invited to go.

When the dancing started I didn't think for a minute about the promise I had made to the Padre. I felt free to enjoy myself because my mother and father were there. When however the day of confession arrived and I was examining my conscience, I was so frightened I decided to say that I had committed an act of disobedience.

Padre Pio opened the grate and the first thing I quickly said was "Father I have disobeyed".

He asked me: "Who have you disobeyed?".

"You father "I answered.

"By doing what?", the Saint asked.

"I danced at a relative's wedding".

The Padre waited a moment and then said: "You acted like

the man who stole a cow. Not to confess the theft as it was he started by saying he had stolen a rope. When the confessor asked him to be a little clearer and give more details, he answered the rope was attached to two horns. At which the confessor bust out laughing, "But don't tell me", he said "you steal horns?". Yes, but the horns belonged to a cow and I took it to my stable".

When the tale was over the Padre said: "You did the same thing. You wanted to pull the wool over Padre Pio's eyes didn't you? You little toad! I'd like to know what pleasure you get from dancing. I've never danced and I have never felt the need to".

So almost to catch my breath, seeing the worst was over I said: "I'd like to see Padre Pio dancing!".

"What are you trying to say? Haven't I been young too?".

He threatened not to give me absolution if ran into that sin again"[91].

Beware of temptation

Jesus, who knows the weakness of human nature, teaches us to pray, turning to the Padre, so that we will not be lead into temptation. Even He who was God, felt the force evil has in reserve and its power is able to damage the soul's power; the apostles felt it during His passion, sifted like wheat. Only the Master's prayer saved them (cf. Lk.22 31-32).

Temptation is to suddenly find oneself at the edge of an abyss: all it takes is a little push from the enemy to fall over; or to be in the eye of a cyclone, exposed to the wind's fury. Only those who are strongly determined to put God in first place and

---

91 Lucietta Pennelli, San Giovanni Rotondo 7.12.1997.

keep their soul in divine grace come out unharmed from the evil that surrounds them.

A spiritual daughter who retired to San Giovanni Rotondo to live near the Saint confides to us: "One day I was walking in the street, when I heard a song. I felt a little nostalgia for the world I had left behind. I quickly acted against this feeling, fighting within my spirit that attraction which had flowered so unexpectedly. I was frightened and threw myself in the arms of Jesus and Our Father.

As soon as I could I told Padre Pio everything that had happened stressing that I had struggled without giving in at all to that temptation. The Padre replied: "That's because your soul is not accustomed to evil, otherwise you would have thrown yourself in the arms of passion"[92].

Looking at politics

Padre Pio advised his spiritual children to be wary about assuming public positions or jobs of responsibility in which economy was involved, even when on their part there was all the good will in the world.

For Christian laity, social involvement is necessary and praiseworthy "When the matter involves discovering or inventing means for permeating social, political and economic realities with the demands of Christian doctrine and life"[93].

History teaches us that power in making decisions regarding public money can be changed into opportunities of danger or sin.

---

[92] *Notes...*, San Giovanni Rotondo, May 1993.
[93] *Catechismo...*, n. 899.

Umberto Di Girolamo worked for the Union. Someone suggested he entered politics. As he was a spiritual son of Padre Pio he wished to hear the Saint's opinion first. He spoke and ended: "Father, in Sicilian there is a saying "If you push me, I'll dive in"".

Padre Pio replied: "My boy, politics teach one to thieve"[94].

Imprudence

Prudence is defined "the virtue that disposes practical reason to discern our true good in every circumstance and to chose the right means of achieving it".

The prudent man "looks where he is going" (Pr 14,15).

The woman who offers the next testimony did not do so and paid dearly for her imprudence, despite having been warned by Padre Pio.

She confesses: "I was young about fifteen or sixteen and longing for a romantic friendship. However I felt a little guilty about it and confessed this to Padre Pio Not knowing how to express how I was feeling I simply said "Father sometimes I am very curious".

The Saint asked for further explanation and I added "Bit by bit as I grow, I want to see, want to feel, want to try things".

Padre Pio as if he were alarmed said: "Beware of curiosity".

I had the sensation that this warning was motivated by some danger the Padre could see.

A few years later a young man took an interest in me. I didn't feel anything for him, but just out of curiosity I started

---

[94] U. Di Girolamo, Trapani 28.10.1996.

to pay him some attention, to see him and to go out with him. At a certain point I started to feel as if I were chained; on one hand I didn't love him and couldn't make wedding plans, on the other I wasn't able to finish with him. In the end I had a nervous breakdown that has marked my life"[95].

Trouble and Sins

Even if we don't experience it personally, we always are surprised and disconcerted in front of the evil in the world, especially if it comes from the abuse of man's freedom. We look back a little naively to the past which seems better than present times.

To the Countess Telfener, who complained one day about how much evil she saw around her, Padre Pio said: "Don't be surprised at anything, there has been, there are and there always will be troubles in this world"[96].

A spiritual daughter affirms "The Father didn't want us to be scandalized facing a person's sins, He encouraged us to make this reflection: "If we do not sin it is only because the Lord keeps us far falling by his grace". Then he added: "The Lord often lets one who is amazed at the sins of others fall into sin themselves"[97].

---

[95]   Dina M., Genova 21.4.1995.
[96]   Rina Giostrelli in Telfener, San Giovanni Rotondo 10.5.1995.
[97]   *Notes…*, San Giovanni Rotondo 8.9.1994.

11. In the arms of God's mercy

We have seen sufficiently, that the Padre was against and strongly warned sinners to leave the road to evil, but humbly knowing his own weakness he urged the penitent to always trust the Heavenly Father's goodness which is full of mercy and forgiveness.

A woman named Giusi was irritated by a woman who called and distracted her whilst she was praying in front of the altar of "Our lady of Grace". A few days later she confessed this to Padre Pio who said: "Come here in front and I'll give you a slap".

She added "Father, I deserve it".

The Saint was surprised by this answer in which she entrusted herself to an immediate judgement. Changing the tone of his voice he said "You stupid woman! Don't you know that if I touch you with only one finger, you won't get up again?" and after a pause "Never say to God "I have sinned and deserve your punishment but rather "Lord I have sinned but be merciful to me. You must have fear, but a confident fear. Remember that"[98].

Padre Pio was moved in front of God's goodness.

A spiritual son tells us that one day, whilst in a lucky moment he was walking in the garden with the Saint speaking of God's tenderness for his creatures, he heard the Saint say: "Don Raffaele, just think about what God is, whilst we are on earth. As an affectionate Father he gives us all if we faithfully turn to him. Even when we offend him and sin, he forgives us, as long as we repent; it would be the same for Judas and the rebel angels. Think if these repented they would be forgiven

---

[98]   Wanda Sellaci, written testimony.

and the earth would be paradise as it once was before"[99].

There are some occasions in life in which we see a rigorous and punitive judgement carried out by God; in the case for example when someone who has not lived a good life dies by accident.

In San Giovanni Rotondo a worker who was always cursing fell from some scaffolding and people saw this as a punishment from God.

What was being said about the accident came to Padre Pio's ears and he was not in agreement about such a rough judgement on the poor man. "Punishment", he said, "is like the reward for our actions, we will only have it in eternity".

Sometimes even death which has not been preceded by a spiritual preparation, accompanied generally by the Sacrament of the sick, can be seen in this light.

Some spiritual children informed Padre Pio that Tina Belloni's brother had fallen from a silo and had mortally crushed to the ground. Tina arrived a few days later at San Giovanni Rotondo and told the Saint of her worries about the salvation of her brother's soul.

The Padre consoled her saying: "It is difficult that a soul not persistently evil, is damned because God at the moment of death appears to the soul and says "do you want me?". The Saint added: "Those who want to go to Hell go there"[100].

Enzo Bertani, claims to have heard Padre Pio say the above phrase more than once[101].

A few spiritual daughters returned to the subject of God's

---

[99]   Dr. Angelo Raffaele Ruzzi Tolve (PZ) 18.10.1986.

[100] *Notes…*, San Giovanni Rotondo, 15 May 1993.

[101] E. Bertani, San Giovanni Rotondo 20.12.1996.

judgement, telling the Padre the general opinion of those who see in the accidents or tragedies that occur a punishment from God.

The Saint replied: "On this earth there is no justice, there is mercy. The painful things are a part of a plan of mercy and love. Justice is up above"[102].

On the same line of thought is the answer the Padre gave to Enzo Bertani, who introduced a mother and father to the Saint. These unhappy parents, full pain for the death of their young son, complained about the tremendous punishment they had received from God".

Padre Pio although he understood their feelings said "You don't know what the Lord saved you from!"[103].

Pietro Cugino tells us that the Padre, when speaking to him, often put God's providence and mercy together. The good blind had the key to the Friary and carried out the little jobs he could do even though he was blind. He ate at he friars' canteen and had a room to sleep in if bad weather prevented him from returning to is home in town. Once he told the Padre of a worry which often returned to trouble him. "Father, as long as you are alive I'm sure there will always be someone to help me with all I need. What will happen to me after your death?".

Padre Pio replied: "That God who helped us yesterday helps us today and will help us tomorrow .He wishes us to abandon ourselves to him. God is love!".

The Saint also repeated to the young man we are unable to do anything, therefore we must put our trust in God and like

---

[102] *Notes…*, San Giovanni Rotondo, May 1993.
[103] *Ibid.*

children have confidence in him. When we feel we can't go on we must say: "Give me a hand". The trouble is we do not pray.

The Padre continued: "We are poor sinners. Let us then try to live in God's presence in the deepest humility. Yes, the Lord wants us to be humble, everyone thinks of a God who judges not as one who loves. If we humble ourselves, God opens his arms to us. The worst thing for us is to distance ourselves from God[104].

Padre Pio feared mercy more than divine justice

The Padre therefore pushed his children to abandon themselves to the arms of God's mercy, however he warned them not to abuse such goodness.

During a break in which the subject was discussed the Saint said to those present "Remember all of you that I have more fear of God's mercy than his justice". After a pause of general silence, he continued saying: "Do you think I have said something wrong? I'll explain quickly the truth of what I said. By means of a penitence, an accepted suffering, an act of pain, a heart felt contrition, I am on a level with the Lord's justice, but with regards to his mercy what can I do? I'd have to live seventy thousand years to give him a minimal part of the mercy that He gives to me"[105].

Padre Pio expressed the same idea in another occasion. He said: "I have more fear of God's mercy than of his justice.

---

[104] Pietro Cugino, San Giovanni Rotondo 2.9.1993.

[105] Fr. Carmelo Durante, Larino (CB) Summer 1986.

God's justice is known: the laws that govern it are known and if one sins and offends his divine justice they can call on his mercy; but if one abuses this, who can they turn to? In this case there is no more remission, because mercy has changed to justice".

He also said: "It is easy to examine what you have done wrong against justice, it is not at all easy to do the same with mercy. How can one say if one matches the great divine mercy?".

Fr. Giustino Gaballo who was present at the discussion exclaimed: "But if we don't even know what the divine mercies we must concern ourselves with are!?".

And the Padre: "Ah, but we do know them. Living is God's mercy, breathing is God's mercy, speaking is God's mercy, understanding is God's mercy and we could continue the list. Now how can we say we have reciprocated all these mercies?".

Then he ended saying "Yes we must dive into the Lord's divine mercy but we mustn't dive into God's goodness without thinking"[106].

The Holy Man also suggested the right method to adopt: "When we stand as sinners before God, we must feel fear and love at the same time: they are two virtues that must go hand in hand. Too much love can harm by making us misuse it, too much fear could distance us from Him".

---

[106] *Chronicle…*, pp. 383. 483-484.

Conclusion

We would like to end this chapter, that has shown us the strictness and moral rigour of Padre Pio, in stigmatizing some sins, taking Gherardo Leone, a spiritual son, as our guide to read in the right key: "The harshness of his reprimands", which came from love.

He writes.

"Padre Pio was not all sweetness. There wasn't a day that went by without him expressing his severity against someone or something, both in and out of Confession. Before some sins he acted instinctively sending the sinner away, because he was so felt so indignant about the sin that had been committed. He was like an archangel on the threshold of Eden, guarding God's laws mercilessly fighting transgressions.

That too was love. He wanted one to know all the beauty of a purified soul. The primordial happiness of being able to look at life and the world through the peaceful eye of a child.

This was what one felt coming out of confession having been absolved by Padre Pio. We felt strong, in harmony with everyone and everything. As if the many things that could trouble us, those blows and counter blows the little and big things of every day life no longer existed.

We were in peace with God. Nothing else mattered, it was no longer there. We felt, at that moment, able to do any heroic gesture, any generous act. It was astounding that all this was given by a man who had lifted his hands to forgive us in the name of the Lord whose imminent, real fatherly presence we felt upon us.

He was also present when the same hand was raised to admonish us and strike us, with the authority of one who is sure of his mandatory power, which was also fatherly because the harshness of the reprimand came from love.

Padre Pio didn't hesitate to pull to pieces, for his behaviour, someone who was not even in Confession, leaving those present astonished and devastated. They were lessons that were for the good of those who received them and those who assisted.

I can really say this, because I too had many reprimands, in public too. They helped me to stop being so cocky: to control my rebellious instinct, my nonchalance in my relationships with others, my lack of bon ton and fair play and a certain way of speaking, inherited from many years lived in the jungle, that didn't take into consideration situations, facts, human relationships not to be underestimated. To sum up, Padre Pio refined me even socially.

Even though I suffered for certain harsh reprimands which left me feeling destroyed (and my friends who had to work hard to cheer me up again, know all about that) I felt as if he was like a father who beat me to correct me for my own good"[107].

Edith Stein, St. Teresa Benedica of the Cross, saw the mission of God's prophets, the saints completely immersed in the Spirit, to whom she sang:

"Are you the spirit's fullness and the power
by which the Lamb releases the seal
of God's eternal decree?
Driven by you the messengers of judgement ride through the world
and separate with a sharp sword
the kingdom of light from the kingdom of night.

---

[107]   GHERARDO LEONE, *Montava la guardia alla Legge del suo Signore*. In *La Casa Sollievo della Sofferenza*, year LIV, N. 3(1-15Feb.2003) 3.

Then Heaven becomes new and new the earth,
and all finds its proper place
through your breath.
Holy Spirit
Victorious power![108].

---

[108]   Edith Stein, *Incontro a Dio…*, 83-84.